TOMMY SIC...

A SENSELESS MURDER

AND THE INDIANAPOLIS POLICE DEPARTMENT

Contents

Chapter One
The Indianapolis Police Department. 1
Chapter Two
The Run to Fred Sanders' House. 19
Chapter Three
What Happens Next?. 40
CHAPTER FOUR
Fred Sanders and the Indianapolis Criminal Courts. 48
CHAPTER FIVE
Civil Rights Lawsuit. U.S. District Court, Indianapolis . . . 62
Attached Figures Below 84
About the Author 91
References 93

TOMMY SICKELS

A SENSELESS MURDER

AND THE INDIANAPOLIS POLICE DEPARTMENT

Copyright © 2024 by Tommy Sickels

All rights reserved. No part of this publication may be reproduced, distributed, or transmitted in any form or by any means, including, photocopying,recording, or other electronic or mechanical methods, without the prior written permission of the copyright owner and the publisher, except in the case of brief quotations embodied in critical reviews and certain other noncommercial uses permitted by copyright law. For permission requests, write to the publisher, addressed "Attention: Permissions Coordinator," at the address below.

CITIOFBOOKS, INC.
3736 Eubank NE Suite A1
Albuquerque, NM 87111-3579
www.citiofbooks.com
Hotline: 1 (877) 389-2759
Fax: 1 (505) 930-7244

Ordering Information:
Quantity sales. Special discounts are available on quantity purchases by corporations, associations, and others. For details, contact the publisher at the address above.

Printed in the United States of America.

ISBN-13:	Paperback	979-8-89391-401-6
	eBook	979-8-89391-402-3

Library of Congress Control Number: 2024921513

A Senseless Murder
and the Indianapolis Police Department

Tommy Sickels

Foreword

The officer's supervisor, Tommy Sickels, tells a true crime story in a book about the Indianapolis Police Department. The text has good explanations of the Indianapolis Police Department structure, history, and specific details of how it functions and operates. Matt Faber was a twenty-four old young man with a lot of life to live. At the time, he had less than two years of service as a police officer with the Indianapolis Police Department. He was married for less than a year and a half to a policewoman. She was hired on the Department about a year before he was; her name is Jan. Matt's assignment was the late-tact shift that began at 7:00 p.m. until 3:00 a.m. The late- tact shift overlapped two other shifts. The afternoon shift starts at 2:00 p.m. until 10:00 p.m. The late shift begins at 10:00 p.m. until 6:00 a.m. The author of this book was a late shift Sergeant. There are Lieutenants and Sergeants assigned to all shifts throughout the city. Because of the overlapping shifts, a late shift Sergeant may have to supervise late-tact shift officers and vice versa.

In this event, Sergeant Sickels receives a radio call to assist officers on a disturbance call regarding a dog. The Sergeant was conducting roll-call for the late shift officers when he received the notification to assist the officers. He finished the roll call and prepared to leave the facility when another broadcast came over the radio. The broadcast told all officers shots were being fired from the location of the original run. The Sergeant finally makes his way to his patrol car and heads toward the site. By the time he got to his car and arrived at the scene, over ten minutes had passed. Sickels could not park near the house. He had to park about a block away and walk up to the location.

The Sergeant noticed more than twenty police cars were on or near the location. Paramedic and fire rescue units were already at the scene. Homicide and robbery detectives were already on the scene. A quick assessment of the situation revealed the following. The primary officer, Matt Faber, had been shot in the back and was lying on the front porch stoop, bleeding profusely. The suspect was lying face down, handcuffed, and two officers were standing beside him. The responding officers were talking with one another. There was an audience of people standing in the street in front of the house. There were at least twenty-five to thirty people watching. At that time Sergeant Sickels realized he would be responsible for completing all departmental reports about this incident.

Detectives were initially charging the suspect with attempted murder and aggravated assault with serious bodily injury. Throughout this reading, you will learn why this case became a travesty of humanity and a farce of the criminal justice system and the Indianapolis Police Department. Within two days, the image of the Indianapolis Police Department took a nosedive. Officers responding to the call to assist Matt Faber were labeled criminals and were conspirators concealing information to hide police brutality and excessive force by employing a 'code of silence' against the suspect, Fred Sanders. Four years after Faber lost his life, you will read the suspect filed a civil rights lawsuit against numerous police officers who were on the scene. Initially, the lawsuit lists thirteen Indianapolis Police Officers as defendants. What were the results of this lawsuit? In the beginning, the prosecutor's office filed murder charges against the suspect. A few days later, the prosecutor filed for the death penalty against Sanders. In the end, he was allowed to plead guilty to a very petty felony crime and served a short time in jail. Sanders did a short time in prison, less than three years. However, the suspect never stepped foot in a prison or jail. He spent time in the Indiana Diagnostic Center in Plainfield, Indiana. The diagnostic center is a rehabilitation center for the mentally ill.

An important issue regarding the Matt Faber run involves a specific police officer responding to the scene. He and another officer made their way to the back door of the house. Upon hearing gunshots, they entered the house from the rear door. Upon seeing the suspect, they left the same way they entered. Later, the prosecutor arrested the primary officer for two misdemeanor crimes. Soon afterward, the Department forced him to resign. His name is Robert Ward Jr. As time passed, several responding officers were transferred or forced to move from their current assignment, some good, but most not good. For some officers it appeared to be career-ending or a dead-end street. It would take many years for the transferred or moved officers to redeem themselves. Another officer, Larry Fender, was charged with police brutality and excessive force against Sanders. A judge finally dismissed the charges. Eventually, most officers returned to their regular previous, except for Fender.

To sum it up, a young police officer was shot in the back and died. Charges of murder would be appropriate in cases of this nature. However, nobody paid the price for Matt Faber's murder. Officers were moved or transferred against their desires. The public made a mockery of the entire police department, making fun of and ridiculing officers in public. The defendant won a large sum of money in a civil rights lawsuit against the police department. One of the police officers gets fired and arrested for unnecessary use of force. But the story never ends for the police department. There is no satisfactory ending to what happened. There will always be officers involved in this case who will never clear the bad taste in their mouths from this incident. Negative issues are surrounding the Matt Faber shooting, and nothing can prevent this from occurring. And to put it all in perspective, the suspect should have talked to Officer Faber in a normal manner. Instead, he decided to argue and run away from the officer.

Chapter One
The Indianapolis Police Department

All readers need to understand this statement. Throughout the text, the author will be referring to the Indianapolis Police Department because that Department was different when the shooting took place. However, the Indianapolis Police Department does not exist today. In 2007 it was abolished and replaced by the Indianapolis Metropolitan Police Department. The Indianapolis Metropolitan Police Department consolidates the Indianapolis Police Department and the Marion County Sheriff's Department. The Indianapolis Police Department was and still is the largest police agency in the State of Indiana. That includes the Indiana State Police. In 1980, the police department had an authorized strength of one thousand three hundred and fifty sworn officers but employed just under one thousand three hundred officers. In addition to the sworn officers, the Department hired more than four hundred and fifty civilian employees. The civilian staff worked in a variety of positions throughout the Department. Some of these positions included 1) Communications Branch. The branch hires radio dispatchers and communication control operators. Dispatchers dispatch police district officers to radio runs. At that time, there were approximately a hundred and fifteen 911 dispatchers. Communication control operators control dispatched district officers while they are on their assigned radio runs. There were two control operators per shift designated for each District. In 1980 there were eight patrol districts. In the Communications Branch, there are fifteen to eighteen 911 call takers per shift. Their job is to screen phone calls and prioritize them for dispatching patrol officers. Consider a patrol district equal to a large city police department consisting of seventy-five to a hundred and fifty police officers.

Over the years, the Indianapolis Police Department has specialized in various areas. Almost all Indianapolis Police Department sections or units have a civilian or two that work as secretaries or

A Senseless Murder and the Indianapolis Police Department

receptionists. The Police Academy is a large organization that runs a full-time staff of civilian and sworn personnel. The Police Radio Station employs more than sixteen personnel. Three of those were officers, and the remainder were civilians. They are responsible for issuing and maintaining the police radios, equipment, and the police radio station. They provide support and service for more than thirteen hundred portable police radios for every police officer in Indianapolis. The Property Branch is responsible for keeping and maintaining any property police officers bring into the Property Room. The Property Branch is open twenty-four hours, seven days a week. It never closes and is staffed with almost all civilian employees. The Crime Lab consists of mainly civilian employees, where some employees must have a Doctorate Degree to operate some of the technical equipment. These are some of the ways the Indianapolis Police Department employs civilian employees.

Today the Indianapolis Police Department has six districts. Each police district has a District Headquarters. There are six of them, they are 1) North, 2) Northwest, 3) Southwest, 4) East, 5) Downtown, 6) Southeast. A District Commander heads each District. The number of officers assigned to a district is dependent on 1) population, 2) geographical size. Five shifts are designated to each District. They are 1) Day – 6 a.m. – 2 p.m., 2) Afternoon – 2 p.m. – 10 p.m., 3) Late – 10 p.m. – 6 a.m., 4) Day-Tact – 9 a.m. – 5 p.m., 5) Late-Tact 7 p.m. – 3 a.m. Each shift has a minimum of one Lieutenant per shift. There are two Sergeants on the day and late shifts and three on the afternoon shift. Both tact shifts have one Sergeant per shift.

Each District has burglary and larceny detectives. The number of detectives depends on the population: The more people, the more detectives. There is a Detective Lieutenant and two Detective Sergeants assigned to each District. Each District has seven to eleven civilian employees depending on the total number of officers assigned. Depending on their needs, there may be one specialized Lieutenant and two to three technical Sergeants assigned to a police district. Each District is unique and has distinctive wants and needs. The District Commander determines these to be successful in fighting crime. Police Districts are variable needing different 'cogs in the machine' to make it run efficiently. What works well in one District may not work in another, vice versa.

Police Headquarters is in Downtown Indianapolis. It is the Grand Central Station for everything that relates or happens to the Indianapolis Police Department. Headquarter houses the Department's leaders and staff. The Department has several Divisions 1) Administration, 2) Investigations, 3) Office of the Chief, 4) Operations. Each Division head is the Division Deputy Chief. A Division has Branches that specialize in individual tasks or jobs. Each Branch head is the Branch Captain. Branches have Sections where Lieutenants head the Sections. Sections have Units where Sergeants run the Branch Units. This example makes it easy to know how the organizational structure is developed for the Indianapolis Police Department. Each Division within the Department follows this guide in terms of developing Branches, Sections, and Units. Today Divisions are called Bureaus. Headquarters houses Major Crimes Branches such as Homicide, Robbery, Auto Theft, Arson, Vice, White Collar Crimes, Sex Crimes, Organized Crimes, Special Investigations, Fugitive Squad, Crime Lab, and Special Investigations. The Investigative Division houses all Major Crimes Branches.

The Administration Division houses these Branches. 1) Property Room, 2) Vehicle Maintenance and Garage, 3) Human Resources, 4) Planning and Research, 5) Training Academy, 6) Firearms Range, 7) UCR Uniform Crime Reporting, and 8) Information Technology – Data Processing. Examples of Branches in the Office of the Chief are 1) Internal Affairs, 2) Data Transcription and Teletype, 3) Assistant Chief's Office, 4) The Police Legal Team, 5) Police Merit Board, 6) Complaint Review Board and 7) Board of Captains. These are some examples that paint a good picture of how the organizational structure is throughout the Department.

Rules and Regulations

All Indianapolis Police Department police officers must follow and abide by the Department's Rules and Regulations Manual. The Rules and Regulations Manual has five sections. 1) Department Rules and Regulations. This section explains what an officer can and cannot do on or off-duty. There are numerous rules and regulations. 2) The Disciplinary Process. Describes how much discipline a police supervisor is authorized to administer for an officer. For example, a Sergeant can suspend an officer without being paid any patrol officer for one day. A Lieutenant can suspend an officer without being paid any Sergeant to patrol officer for up to two days. A Captain can suspend an officer without paying any Lieutenant, Sergeant, or patrol officer for up to three days. Majors, Assistant Commanders, Deputy Chiefs, or the Assistant Chief of Police can suspend anyone below their rank without pay for four days up to ten days.

The Police Merit Board

The Chief of Police can suspend any Indianapolis Police Department officer without pay for one day up to six months or recommend termination. No matter the rank of the officer recommending discipline, all officers (except for probationary officers) are entitled to due process. Any officer recommended for any discipline matter may appeal to the Police Merit Board. The Police Merit Board conducts an administrative hearing. The Merit Board has subpoena powers and calls witnesses or complainants. The hearing follows the rules of court procedure. If an officer disagrees with the Merit ' Board's decision, they may appeal to the Marion County Superior Court and hope for better outcomes.

There are other less severe forms of discipline. 1) Written Reprimand. Used when an officer violates any rule or regulation that is less than egregious. Any suspension or written reprimand affirmed becomes a permanent record filed in the officer's personnel file. 2) Counseling Form. Supervisors use this form when an officer makes a minor violation of any Department rule or regulation. The Counseling Form is not a permanent record, and the Department will destroy the form in twelve months unless the officer commits the same violation in less than twelve months.

The Police Merit Board regulates all promotional processes. The Indianapolis Police Department administers promotional tests for the following ranks: Sergeant, Lieutenant, and Captain. These tests are conducted every two to three years. The Department will establish eligibility lists that expire in two years. Promotions must come from the lists and must be in top-down order. These promotions require a one-year probationary period, after which time the rank becomes permanent. The Chief of Police has the authority to assign 'appointed ranks.' They include Major, Assistant Commander, Commander, Deputy Chief, and Assistant Chief. The Chief of Police will appoint officers to these ranks, and they serve at the pleasure of the Chief. There is no merit to the appointment, and they are not permanent. These positions are known as the 'Chief's Staff.'

Rules and Regulations

Rules and Regulations are those that apply to the Indianapolis Police Department. Rules and regulations refer to the 'dos and don'ts' of the Department. Generally, these are things you can do and cannot do as a police officer for the Indianapolis Police Department. In this manual, there are various policies, statements, processes, and boards to review. These are a few examples. Mission Statement – committed to creating and maintaining active police/ community partnerships and dedicated to upholding the highest professional standards. Police Officers' Bill of Rights – Explains an officer's rights regarding internal investigations, criminal charges, disciplinary matters, and similar subjects. The disciplinary process. The Disciplinary Board of Captains. The Complaint Review Board and their statutory authority. Internal Affairs and their investigative power. What can Internal Affairs do and not do during and after an investigation? Examples of a few rules and regulations are below.

Examples of Indianapolis Police Department Rules and Regulations

1. "Members shall report for duty at the assigned time and place with all necessary equipment and properly attired to perform their duties.
2. Members shall devote full time to their duties during the time they are working for the department.
3. Members shall not engage in any activities or personal business which would cause them to be inattentive to duty.
4. Members shall not leave their assigned duty unless properly relieved or by permission of a supervisor, or unless authorized to do so by Communications.
5. Members shall not sleep while on duty.
6. Members shall not feign illness or injury, falsely report themselves ill or injured, or otherwise deceive or attempt to deceive any official of the department as to the condition of their health.
7. Members shall report for duty at the time and place required by assignment or orders and shall be physically and mentally fit to perform their duties" (Rules and Regulations Manual, Rules and Regulations Manual, 2009).

General Orders

General Orders is the Department's SOP (Standard Operating Procedures) manual. The General Orders manual is a three-ringed blue binder that recruit trainees receive in the Police Academy. According to the Department's rules and regulations, officers shall keep and maintain General Orders and keep the manual current with the most recent updates. When an officer retires, the General Orders Manual is returned to the Chief's Office as part of their returned equipment.

The General Orders Manual is more than five hundred pages and contains more than one hundred and seventy General Orders. Over time, every task an officer performs has been reviewed, critiqued, and reevaluated. This example shows where the origin of the General Orders began. See Figure 7, General Order 1.1. The General

Orders Manual has codified every task performed by officers of the Indianapolis Police Department. A detailed description of each task has 'how-to' instructions for completing the job. There are illustrations and photos in some of the general orders. The manual is indexed by General Order number and in alphabetical order. The Department continuously updates general orders and distributes the updates to all officers. Officers shall replace the old general order with the updated version. The Department Rules and Regulations manual is inside the General Orders Manual.

So, You Want to Become an Indianapolis Police Officer?

Requirements: Making application to be a cop at the Indianapolis Metropolitan Police Department, applicants must:

- Be a U.S. citizen
- Be at least twenty-one years old and younger than thirty-six
- Have a high school diploma or GED
- Have a valid driver's license
- Be a resident of Marion County, Indiana, or one of the seven adjoining counties. Note: (Only after hired. Applicants can live anywhere in the United States to qualify for application.) Note by author.
- Not have any misdemeanor convictions of domestic violence
- Not have ever been arrested for or convicted of a felony
- Not have been dishonorably discharged from the military ("How To Become A Police Officer", Website).

If you read this section, you will realize it is not easy to become an Indianapolis police officer. Applicants must compete with hundreds of applicants for a limited number of openings. The hiring process is time- consuming and drags on for six to eight months. All pre-employment phases are competitive. The Police Department will eliminate applicants for Police Recruit Trainee for those not passing any stage of the pre- employment process.

When reading through the book, several Indianapolis police officers are characters within the text. It is important to remember anyone mentioned in this book had to go through this process to become a police officer. Also, these individuals had to pass the Academy and FTO training. Not an easy task. It's not an easy job and sometimes thankless. There are always people who criticize anybody, no matter what the circumstances are. Recruit classes have forty to sixty trainees. All of those trainees had to beat more than fourteen hundred applicants applying for the same job. Someone had to do something right to get the job as Indianapolis Police Officer.

Becoming an Indianapolis police officer can be a difficult task. The Department hires at least one recruit class each year. Newly hired Police Recruit Trainees attend the Indianapolis Police Department Academy. The Indiana Law Enforcement Training Board approves the curriculum and all training standards for the State of Indiana. Training Board members assist in the development of every class. The class schedule can be challenging and rigorous, requiring demanding study skills. Physical activity can be too hard for some trainees and may cause their demise. Courses consist of academic, hands-on, clinical, and scenario-based training. Physical exercise can deplete the best-trained individuals and may cause some trainees to resign. The Academy is not a residence-based training facility. Trainees are not required to live in the Academy. They report daily and leave after eight to ten hours each day, Monday through Friday. To graduate from the Indianapolis Police Academy takes six months. The location of the Indianapolis Police Academy is at East 10th Street and Post Road on the east side of Indianapolis.

The Department accepts sign-ups every day of the year. For recruit classes, there is a 'sign-up cut-off date' that stops the sign-up period. The cut-off date halts sign-ups, and a new list begins for the next recruit class.

he Department likes to sign-up thirteen to fifteen hundred individuals per list. Each person on the sign-up list will receive a notice of the written examination's date, time, and location. Only fifty percent of those taking the written test are allowed to pass. The physical agility is next. A minimal number of applicants fail the agility test. Those that pass the agility test will be going in front of the interview panel. Again, only fifty percent of the interviewees were allowed to pass the interview. There will be approximately ninety to a hundred and twenty applicants remaining. Those applicants will undergo an extensive background investigation. Those who survive the background investigation will go to the polygraph examination. After the polygraph phase, there will be anywhere from forty to sixty applicants remaining. They will receive a "conditional offer of employment." The condition is to pass a physical examination and mental evaluation required by the Indiana Police and Fire Pension Board. A very few do not pass these tests. Those passing the conditional offer will be hired as Indianapolis Police Recruit Trainees.

Indianapolis Police Pay

In 1986, pay for the Indiana police officers was much different than it is today, 2021. In 1986 starting pay for recruit trainees was around 22,000 dollars. The trainee will receive that pay until they become a patrolman first class. Patrolman first class begins one year after officers graduate from the Police Academy. The pay raises to 25,000 dollars. In another two years, three years after graduating from the Police Academy, the pay increases to 28,500 dollars. The Department refers to this as patrol officers' 'base pay.' Officers working afternoon, late tact, and late shifts receive an additional 80 cents per hour. It is called 'shift premium' pay. All officers, regardless of their assignment, receive 600 dollars per year for a clothing allowance. Motorcycle patrol, horse patrol, and SWAT officers receive 600 dollars per year for hazard duty pay. Canine officers receive an additional 50 cents per hour for special duty pay. However, these officers work seven hours each day instead of eight because they receive extra time off for dog maintenance.

When off duty, officers going to court get a minimum of two hours' pay for anything under two hours spent in court. They will be paid by the hour if they are in court for more than two hours until they leave the court. Sergeants earn fifteen percent more than the base pay of third-year patrolmen. Lieutenants earn fifteen percent more than a Sergeant. Captains make fifteen percent more than a Lieutenant. Detectives earn $1,400 per year more than their rank while they are detectives. All officers enjoy longevity pay which begins three years after graduating from the Police Academy. Each year longevity pay increases by a half percent per year. Regardless of rank, all residual income is the same for all officers.

The last thing regarding Indianapolis Police Department pay. College incentive pay began in the mid-1970s. Since its inception, the incentive pay has remained the same and has never changed. No increases, nothing has happened. It is the same. The guess is easy to conclude as there is not much interest in the college incentive pay program. Officers that have a bachelor's degree will receive a thousand dollars per year. Those with master's or doctoral degrees will not receive any extra pay. Those degrees are worthless. Every 30 credit hour increment (or equivalent) an officer earns toward a bachelor's degree is worth two hundred and fifty dollars a year up to 90 credit hours or seven hundred and fifty dollars. An officer can earn 120 credit hours or more, but they will not receive the thousand dollars if they do not complete the bachelor's degree. Most bachelor's degrees require 120 credit hours. An officer can earn 130 credit hours or more and not complete a bachelor's degree. This would be an example of poor planning.

The Hiring Process

All rules and regulations govern the hiring process for the Indianapolis Police Department. Rules and Regulations explain the Chief's authority to hire police officers. The Merit Board ratifies the hiring eligibility list, and Indiana laws govern the Police Merit Board hiring practices. By law, the eligibility list can be active for up to one year. The Merit Board approves all pre-employment hiring phases they are 1) written test, 2) physical agility test, 3) oral interviews, 4) background investigation, 5) physical examination, 6) psychological exam and interview with the police psychiatrist.

The Written Test

Over the years, challenges to the written exam have caused the test to change from an academic achievement test to a law enforcement-related exam. Before the test date, the Department must provide an opportunity for a pre-test study session. Because there are too many applicants taking the written test, more than fourteen hundred, only fifty percent of those taking the test can pass. Rank order is top-down exam scores. Tiebreakers, there are many ways to break a tie score. If fifteen people have the same score, the chief tiebreaker is a college education. A person that has the highest education level and downward. From Ph. D. to master's degrees and bachelor's degrees. Those with a major in criminal justice, justice administration, police administration, or similar law enforcement-related fields will receive a better rating than those with a degree in basket weaving or hopscotch. These are followed by those who did not complete their degree. Irrespective of a degree, that person will receive a slightly better rating than those who have nothing. The more credit or semester hours toward the degree, the better the rating will result. Other written test score tie-breakers include the date of sign-up. Sign-up begins on January 1st and ends on July 30th. Applicants who are signing up on January 1st will be selected first, and so on.

Oral Interview Board

The oral interview board is an essential process for applicant screening. Every applicant receives the same interview. There are no secret or hidden interview questions. Interviews have a maximum time limit of twenty minutes. There is no minimum time limit. There are numerous interview boards, somewhere around eight or nine boards. Each interview board consists of six members. The members consist of three patrol officers, a sergeant, a lieutenant, and a captain. Each member asks an applicant one question each. There are six interview questions. Applicants cannot spend more than three and a half minutes answering each question. Interview Board members receive training on how to grade interviews since they attend a four-hour seminar on grading structured interviews

The Physical Agility Test

The test measures an applicant's physical abilities in a variety of physical tasks. There are various tasks included in the agility test. Such as the mile and a half run, crossing over a five-foot wall, balance beam, trigger pull, brake reaction-time test, pulling a 125-pound dummy thirty feet less than fifteen seconds. A person who fails one of these tasks fails the physical agility test. There is a tiebreaker to this test, and that is the date of sign-up. The closer to the sign-up start date will bring better results. Those with law enforcement experience will break up ties, and they will move further up the list. Sergeant Dale Ferguson was the coordinator of the pre-employment process and scheduled all applicant screening tests. He was a significant assistant in the agility test. Because of his efforts, very few applicants failed the agility test because of his coaching and positive reinforcement.

Background Investigation

The Human Resources Branches Background Investigation Unit conducts the background investigations. The process will take approximately three months to complete. The Background Investigation Unit consists of seven to ten patrol officers and one sergeant. These officers must complete the detective training school and successfully pass a screening process for the position. The investigation itself is comprehensive. Investigators examine numerous areas of concern: 1) credit history, 2) past and current employment history, including a discussion with the ' applicant's current supervisor, 3) neighborhood canvass talking to neighbors of the applicant, 4) reference check—the references used by the applicant, 5) home visit will include an interview with the spouse, parents or partner, 6) education status check. Those passing the background investigation will go to the polygraph test.

Polygraph – Lie Detector Test

The Indianapolis Police Department conducts lie detector tests to eliminate individuals as applicants. While the applicant is taking the test, the polygraphist will continuously evaluate the test. Applicants who admit to committing crimes, violating social or moral norms, stealing from past employers, cheating on their income taxes or spouse, engaging in drug trafficking or its use, or other related subjects will fail the test. Applicants fail the polygraph test because of their admission to questions or a specific question during the polygraph test. These are a few confession examples applicants have made. The applicant worked for a national appliance chain store. He started by taking photocopy paper and small office supplies that did not amount to much money. Then he moved to small to medium size printers or VHS movies, then computer monitors. It progressed to stealing televisions, washers, dryers, and stereo systems. Another applicant admitted to watching a lady in a Kroger Store parking lot loading groceries into her car. Then, following the lady to her house, he watched her unload the groceries and go inside her house. After waiting ten or more minutes, he walked up to the house and began peeking into the windows. He saw her inside a bedroom undressing and started masturbating. Needless to say, the Indianapolis Police Department did not hire these individuals. Background investigators must view some polygraph tests in a 'view room' next to the polygraphist.

Physical Examination

The appointed police physician does the physical exams on all police applicants. The standards required must meet the Indiana Pension' Board's recommendations. Applicants can fail the exam for various reasons. Some of them are high blood pressure, overweight or underweight, eliminating heart condition, or any severe or life-threatening disease or illness, or history of mental illness. Some applicants who have less intense physical conditions may pass the exam if they sign a waiver that exempts the health condition as a cause of early pension. Meaning they will not receive a pension if the illness was the cause of early retirement. The key is early retirement. The person can retire if they meet the standard requirement of retirement.

Mental Health Evaluation

The Indianapolis Police Department Psychiatrist conducts this process. It consists of two tests. Both tests are a requirement of the Indiana Police and Fire Pension Board. The two tests are 1) MMPI, the Minnesota Multi- Phasic Inventory test. A four hundred and seventy-eight multiple-choice question test takes approximately an hour and a half to complete. 2) Review of the MMPI and interview with the Psychiatrist. The Psychiatrist will interview each applicant after they have evaluated the MMPI results. The Psychiatrist will inform the test takers about the results of their exam in writing.

The Indianapolis Police Department will hire all applicants that pass these phases of the screening process. The Department will offer each applicant the 'recruit trainee' position in the police department. They will attend the Police Academy for twenty-five weeks and will go through twenty weeks of field training. Every trainee who passes the training will attend the Academy graduation after the field training phase.

The Academy will assign five different FTOs (Field Training Officers) to each trainee for twenty weeks. Trainees will spend four weeks with each FTO. Every day the FTO evaluates the trainee. The FTO will use the same evaluation form every day. Over time, it becomes a bit repetitive and redundant. However, the daily evaluations do serve a purpose, which is to weed out unqualified Recruit Trainees. Every Academy class has at least one trainee that does not survive, if not more from FTO training. A few of the Recruit

Trainees quit or resigned during the Academy phase of their training. If recruit Trainees cannot make it through the Academy or the FTO training phase, they cannot become Indianapolis Police Officers. The Department will fire these people.

Trainees successfully completing Academy and FTO training will receive their 'full-duty status.' Their full duty status will be posted on the Academy bulletin board. The full duty status shows recruits where they will permanently be assigned as probationary officers. Trainees will have a few days off before they begin working their permanent assignments. They must attend the Class Graduation. The Mayor and other dignitaries of the city government will be attending. All graduating class members should have their family and relatives attend. Graduation from the Indianapolis Police Academy is a once-in-a-lifetime experience. It's also an excellent photo-taking opportunity.

Once the Recruit Trainee graduates from the Academy, they will never be called "a trainee" again. They are full-fledged police officers. All new officers will report to the police vehicle maintenance garage and have their police car assigned. Each officer will be assigned a "take-home"' police car. The officer can drive the vehicle when they are off-duty. The officer may go into any contiguous county touching Marion County, Indiana. There are eight adjacent counties. The city will deduct forty dollars a month from the ' officer's pay for gas. Officers not wishing to have the deduction will not be allowed to drive the car while off duty. After the new officers receive their vehicles, they will report to the Radio Station to receive their portable radios. The radio is standard equipment for all Indianapolis police officers. They will receive a portable radio and a charger. According to Department rules, while officers use a police car on or off duty, they shall have the portable radio and sidearm accessible in the police car. There are no exceptions to this rule. Officers violating this rule may receive monetary discipline if found guilty.

A new officer reporting to their duty assignment for the first time can be stressful. Most new officers are welcomed by the senior officers and supervisors. They are welcome because the veteran officers appreciate their presence. The presence of newly assigned officers helps ease the workload a bit, and the senior officers know this to be a fact. New officers work alone. Working alone became an Indianapolis tradition in 1969 when it became the first municipal government to assign "take-home" police cars in the United States. The Indianapolis Police Department started this pilot project to save the city tax dollars in vehicle maintenance.

Patrolman First Class

While a full duty status officer is new to the Department, they must spend one year as a probationary officer. Probationary officers enjoy limited job security during the probationary period. The probationary period starts the day after recruit trainees graduate from the Police Academy and lasts one year after graduation. Limited job security means the Department can terminate or discipline probationary officers without "due process." After the probationary period, the officer becomes a "Patrolman First Class." These officers have "due process" protection from the Department and the supervisory staff. Due process comes with different meanings. In the most tangible sense, it means an officer cannot arbitrarily be fired or disciplined by the Chief of Police or any supervisor without "due process." The officer can challenge firings or disciplinary matters without the approval of the Board of Captains. Officers that disagree with the Board of Captain's decision can appeal their case to the Police Merit Board. An appeal to the Merit Board is through an administrative hearing. If the Merit Board affirms the firing or disciplinary matter, the officer may appeal their decision to the Marion County Superior Court. In Indiana, an administrative hearing is akin to a court trial with rules, regulations, and subpoena powers, much like a court. The Superior Court has the final word, and their decision is final. It is the stopping point regarding administrative disciplinary procedures.

Police Cars and Portable Radios

In just over a year, the city noticed it saved more than a million dollars in police car maintenance alone. In 1969 the Indianapolis Police Department began a take-home police car program. During the late 1970s, the program expanded city-wide. Indianapolis was the first municipal police agency to start this type of program in the United States. All Indianapolis police officers were assigned a take-home police car regardless of their assignment. Indianapolis benefited from the program in various ways 1) Police Vehicle maintenance versus the twenty-four hours a day (hot seat cars). 'Hot seat' cars were the standard for the city and all across America. Police cars were purchased every twelve months, sometimes less. Since the take-home program began, cars have been purchased every four to five years. 2) Police presence. Police cars were everywhere; therefore, the city of Indianapolis's benefit was crime deterrence and prevention. 3) Mobility of all officers regardless of their assignment. 4) Deploying. SWAT, Special Weapons, and Tactic officers became seamless after the take-home car program. SWAT officers were able to deploy within a matter of minutes as opposed to more than an hour.

The police radio system employed by the Department was the best money could buy. The portable radios were from the General Electric Company, and many departments across America were using the same system. Again, only one officer per portable radio. The radios, like the police cars, had an excellent maintenance program and record. The General Electric portable radio system was in use for more than twelve years. The Department switched to a newer and more efficient Motorola Radio system. Motorola radios have gone through replacement and updates, but the same radio system is employed today. Portable radios are like police cars. Officers do not share portable radios. Radios will last longer and perform better with one user compared to multiple users. By 1990 the entire radio system changed Department-wide.

Marion County government created a new agency to oversee communications for the Indianapolis Police Department and the Marion County Sheriff's Department. The new agency took control of the Radio Station, communications center, and dispatchers. This agency was called MECA, Metropolitan Emergency Communication Administration. However, in 2012 MECA was replaced by the Sheriff of Marion County. He is in charge of county-wide communications. Today there are more than five hundred and thirty 911 dispatches, supervisors, radio station personnel, and whatever it takes to run the communications center. It is an efficiently run organization using all of the best and current state-of-the-art equipment in radio communications in America.

Chapter Two
The Run to Fred Sanders' House

August 14th, 1988 at 9:21 p.m., police received a call to see Perry W. Evans 2961 Arthington Blvd regarding a man who lives across the street. The man has a dog he ordered to bite Perry Evans' children. The dog chased Perry's children around the block, but the dog did not bite them. Perry wanted the police to talk to the man to have him stop the dog. Sergeant Kent Knap provided this information. Matt Faber told Knap the following about the suspect, Fred C. Sanders, forty-four years of age, 2968 Arthington Blvd lives across the street from Perry Evans' home. Faber related to Sergeant Knap that Perry W. Evans, twenty-four, told him that Fred Sanders ordered his dog to attack the children of Evans who were playing in the street. Faber also told Sergeant Knap that Sanders had several guns in his house and fired a gun at his home earlier in the year.

In an article written by the *Indianapolis Star* newspaper, a lot of what Matt Faber told Sergeant Knap was true. George McClaren, a newspaper staff writer, authored a story that states, Faber was answering a call about a man allowing his dog to chase children. The dog chased Evans' child while he was riding a scooter. Evans called for the police. When Officer Faber arrived, Evans told the officer the man (Sanders) had guns in his house. Faber asked Evans, "How do you know he has guns?" Evans responded, "How do I know he has guns? He's shot in my house before," he said. Another neighbor supported the claim Sanders' dogs were a menace. She said, "All I know was about some dogs. They're always chasing people, the dogs are," said the woman, who asked not to be identified. (McClaren, August 15, 1988).

Faber continued the conversation with Perry Evans as a routine matter. Causing a dog to chase a child riding a scooter requires a police report. Officers shall make a police report anytime a person causes bodily injury or threat by attempting to cause physical injury to another person. Matt Faber's conversation with Evans was to gather information for a police report. A report of this type would require Perry Evans' entire descriptive profile to include age, date of birth, social security number, address, location of the incident, telephone number, and the time the incident occurred. The victim information, in this case, Perry's young son was the victim. His descriptive information is a requirement for the report, just as his father's. Any witness and their descriptive information must accompany the police report. Witnesses must have seen the event take place. Completing a police report, officers shall summarize what happened, who the victim is, and what they said. Who the witnesses are and what they saw. The last thing in a police report is to include a suspect. Faber should provide any information regarding a suspect and their descriptive profile.

Officers learn while in the Police Academy to use their 'field notebook' as a report tablet. Later the notebook is a reference while the officer completes the incident report form. Officers have the option to turn the report over to the Teletype Branch, where operators will enter the report information into the reporting system. Or they may choose to telephone call the report to a dictating system where teletype operators can enter the data into the reporting system. What happens to these reports? While in the Police Academy, instructors teach recruit trainees if a report seems like it will generate criminal charges, they instruct the complainant to contact the detectives. Officer Faber would tell Perry Evans to get in touch with the East District detectives. All Indianapolis police reports are printed at 6:00 a.m. sorted and delivered to the appropriate District, Branch, Unit, or Section of the Department. Detective supervisors read every report coming to their office and assign cases to detectives as needed.

None of this occurred in Fred Sanders' run. Sergeant Sickels found Matt Faber's field notebook in his shirt pocket. He saw where Faber entered the descriptive profile of Perry Evans but did not see anything else about this incident. Anything beyond what was in the notebook would be speculation or guesswork. When officers take report information, they first talk to the complainant, who made the call to the police. Second, officers want to speak to "who they are complaining about?" Officers do this to get the opposite side of the story. It is better to have both sides of a story. One-sided stories tend to be subjective, but it depends on the facts. Perry Evans said Officer Faber wanted to talk to Fred Sanders. Faber crossed the street and headed toward Sanders' yard, where he was standing.

Fred Sanders was standing in his front yard while Faber was talking to Perry Evans. Faber obtained the personal information of Evans. Officers are required to maintain a field notebook. The notebook is a tablet used to jot down information needed for police reports. Sergeant Sickels took the field notebook from Officer Faber's shirt pocket. Faber told Evans he would talk to Mr. Sanders and file a police report. As all police officers learn in training, they tell crime victims to call a district detective to seek further information about the police report. The detective will advise victims if criminal charges are forthcoming. Matt noticed a dog pen in Sanders' side yard. The dog pen is about a five-by-five-foot fenced-in area. Faber noticed there were three dogs inside the enclosure at the time of his arrival. As Faber engaged in discussion with Sanders, he asked, 'am I under arrest?' Faber replied, 'at this time, no.' Both of them were near the sidewalk in front of Sanders' home. Sanders immediately turned around and walked towards the front door. Perry Evans overheard the conversation between Faber and Sanders.

Faber told Sanders to stop walking, but he refused. Faber approached Sanders and tapped him on the shoulder, and asked him to stop. Sanders turned around and pushed Faber away and continued walking toward the door. Matt immediately called for assistance to the Sanders location. Several officers close by, including Sergeant Knap and Larry Fender, responded quickly. Faber continued to thwart Sanders' movement to the front door, but he was unsuccessful. Sanders was a huge man outweighing Faber by two times. Faber told Sanders he was under arrest for resisting law enforcement, but the resistance continued. Sergeant Knap and Officer Fender arrived and noticed Sanders and Faber very close to the front door. Before Sergeant Knap and Officer Fender show up, Fred Sanders becomes belligerent with Faber, calling him names and expressing many vulgar words. Then he starts cussing across the street, saying the

N-word while making numerous racial slurs to neighbors. Sanders continues this behavior until Knap and Fender arrive at the front door.

A Scuffle at the Front Door

As the two officers approached the front door, Sanders managed to close the door in front of Faber. However, the front door did not close completely. Faber worked his foot between the door edge and door frame, stopping the door from completely closing. By this time, Sergeant Knap and Officer Fender were at the front door. Larry was one of the three officers at the front door of Fred Sanders' house. During this melee of events that took more than five minutes, a very dynamic situation occurred amongst the three officers, Faber, Knap, and Fender. The three officers continued to trade positions and places with each other as if they were in a dance. Faber told Knap and Fender, 'Fred Sanders may have guns in the house.' The struggle continued as all three officers were pushing against the door, attempting to force it open. The activity at the front door was like a dog fight, a very disorganized scuffle taking place with very little organization. Little or nothing seemed to occur as the officers weren't getting anywhere, no progress, and it seemed like an eternity for the three officers.

The scuffle between Sanders and the three officers is becoming a battle of strength and the door. The door becomes partially open, and Officer Fender managed to get his arm into the other side of the door to spray his C.S. repellant on Fred Sanders. C.S. repellant is a skin irritant that significantly makes the skin feel as it were on fire. The C.S. repellant did not affect Sanders in any way. He continued to push against the door. Sergeant Knap began to lead the charge at the door as he managed to use his baton, swinging it at Sanders' arm and shoulder. Again, this maneuver did not affect the actions of Sanders. Using the baton on Sanders had absolutely no effect on his actions. Sanders continued pushing against the door keeping the officers at bay without interruption.

The struggle became futile because it seemed the officers could not do anything to gain entry through the doorway. It became a full-fledged battle between the three officers and Fred Sanders. World

War III in front of the Sanders residence in Indianapolis, Indiana. It was a sweltering evening, ninety-one-plus degrees causing officers to sweat profusely. When Sergeant Sickels arrived, he noticed their uniforms were wet, soaked with sweat.

The struggle between the officers and Sanders changes dimensions again with Officer Faber taking the lead role. He was first in line while Fender and Knap were behind him. All three were pushing the door against Sanders. Suddenly and without notice, the front door opened abruptly and quickly. The quick opening caused a domino effect of the officers going through the doorway. Since Officer Faber was in the front position and the other officers were behind him, all three abruptly went through the doorway. Being the first officer through the door, Faber grabbed Sanders, but he was so sweaty that his hands slipped off him, and all officers fell to the floor. Both Knap and Fender were able to get up to their feet quickly. Faber was still lying on the floor, struggling to get up. Fender and Knap noticed Sanders was not present in the living room. He had disappeared. Knap and Fender heard what appeared to be the sound of a shotgun cocking, and they saw Sanders appearing in the kitchen, aiming a shotgun towards them.

Knap and Fender both said they saw Faber on the floor, turning around getting on his knees. As he was upright on his knees, they saw Sanders take about three or four steps from the kitchen toward Faber and fired a single shot at his back. Knap said Sanders was no more than a foot away from Faber when he made the shot. The blast hit the upper left portion of Faber's back. Faber immediately fell facedown to the floor.

Fender and Knap moved to the porch stoop and stood behind the front of the house. Fender was on one side of the doorway, while Knap was on the other side. Just moments after, Knap and Officer Fender fired their guns at Sanders at two different times. Both were standing at the front door on the porch stoop. As they saw Sanders hiding behind a wall in the kitchen, he appeared briefly, and they both fired at him as he ducked behind the wall. Sanders reappeared again, and they fired a second time at him. A few seconds after the second volley of gunshots, both officers knew Sanders was struck by their bullets but were unsure of his injuries. Sanders hid behind the wall and did not come out. At that time, he was quiet and did not say anything.

Sergeant Knap was able to talk with Sanders, asking him to give up. It got to a point when Knap told Sanders, [sic] "give up because you are under arrest for shooting Officer Faber in the back, resisting arrest and disorderly conduct." Sanders did not respond or acknowledge any of Knap's comments. It was like Sergeant Knap did not exist. To Sanders, Knap wasn't there, as he did not say a word. Sort of like talking to a stone, as if you are talking to nothing. But a couple of seconds later, Sanders put the shotgun on the floor and walked toward the door, giving up.

As Sanders walked outside onto the porch stoop, he saw Sergeant Knap standing nearby. When he got close to Knap, Sanders pushed him and knocked him down into a bush beside the porch. Officers already on the scene assisted in handcuffing Fred Sanders. They grabbed Sanders and pushed him down in the front yard to handcuff him. First, they tried one set of handcuffs, but they were too short. They were not able to get his hands behind his back close enough to handcuff him. They had to chain-link two pairs of handcuffs together to make them longer; this maneuver worked. These events occurred before Sergeant Sickels arrived at the Sanders residence. He never saw any of these events take place.

The communications center broadcasts shots fired at the Sanders residence, and Officer Faber is the shooting victim. Numerous officers, supervisors, and detectives, as well as paramedics, converged to the scene. These events occurred while Sergeant Sickels oversaw the late shift roll call at the East District Headquarters on East 30th Street. Paramedics transported Fred Sanders to Wishard Memorial Hospital, where he was treated for his injuries. The hospital staff informed Sergeant Sickels, Mr. Sanders' injuries were not severe and would not require long-term treatment.

Sergeant Sickels Arrives at Sanders Residence

Sergeant Sickels arrived at the Sanders location but had to park his police car a block away from Arthington Blvd. As Sickels walks up to the residence, he observes a large crowd standing in front of the Sanders residence. Sergeant Sickels also sees numerous police officers and supervisors, detectives, and paramedic units on the scene. As Sickels walks into the front yard of Sanders' residence, he observes Fred Sanders lying face down next to a tree in the middle of the yard. Officers handcuffed Sanders from the back. Fred Sanders was a large man, officers who handcuffed him had to chain-link two pairs of handcuffs behind his back. Sergeant Sickels caught a view of Officer Faber lying face down on the front porch stoop. It was a concrete slab about six-by-six feet. Faber was bleeding from the back, bleeding profusely. He was in a great deal of pain, calling out for help. At the time, sweat was pouring from his face onto the concrete slab. It was running like a water faucet. From Faber's appearance and demeanor, Sickels was able to tell that he wanted help and relief from the pain and suffering.

Several officers were standing in front of Faber, encouraging him to fight the pain. They were saying, 'Come on, Matt, you can make it. Don't give up; keep fighting.' The officers' chants did not stop as they continued encouraging Matt. It did not stop until the ambulance took Faber from the scene to the hospital. When the ambulance left, a few encouraging officers did not know how to react to what they witnessed. A few were angry, while others expressed sadness from what happened. To Sergeant Sickels, he was just as confused as the officers who were chanting encouragement. He, too, wanted Matt to pull through the trauma he was suffering; he was in severe distress. To be honest, Matt did not appear to respond to anything the officers were saying because he was in so much pain. The events on the porch stoop had a profound effect on the officers at the scene. Most officers could not believe what transpired because Sanders allowed his dog to chase children in the neighborhood.

One thing officers learned when paramedics began to work Faber shocked their consciousness. He was not wearing his department-issued 'bulletproof vest.' Why? Later through a conversation with Jan Faber, Matt did not wear the vest because it was too hot. Wearing the vest does create more body heat. Could it have made a difference from the shotgun blast? Yes, but what kind of difference? A .12 gauge shotgun blast with a bulletproof vest would have absorbed the shot.

A Senseless Murder and the Indianapolis Police Department

The impact from the blast would cause significant impact trauma because the shotgun blast was from a very close range. If Matt had worn the vest, it would have protected him because a bulletproof vest covers the front and back sides. Where the shotgun hit him in the back was where the vest would have been. Wearing or not wearing the vest is a matter of speculation, and in the final analysis, not wearing the vest was never discussed among department members.

In talking to Sergeant Knap, it was evident he was directly involved in the shooting firing his gun toward Fred Sanders. He was the tact-shift Sergeant responsible for completing all special reports on his shift. Sergeant Knap told Sergeant Sickels, 'the struggle at the door probably took four to five minutes but seemed like an eternity. It looked like everything slowed down to a crawl and took forever.' Because Sergeant Knap was directly involved in the officer-involved shooting, he could not complete the Department's special reports. Sergeant Sickels had to take on the responsibility. Special departmental reports required for this case are. 1) Initial Incident Report 2) C.S. Repellant Usage 3) Officer Assaulted Report. Three reports are needed; a) Knap, b) Faber, c) Fender, 4) Officer Injured Report. Three reports are required. a) Faber, b) Ward, c) Fender, 5) Resisting Arrest Report. 6) Inter-departmental report. The reports summarized everything occurring during the incident, forwarded it to the Chief of Police. These special reports were completed later that evening by Sergeant Sickels (see completed special report forms at the end of this book).

Paramedics transported Officer Faber to Wishard Hospital emergency room from Sanders' location. Faber had internal bleeding while surgeons performed emergency surgery to repair the damage. When the surgery was over, hospital transporters moved Faber to the intensive care unit. The intention was Faber would stay there until he recuperated from his wound. The hospital staff put Faber in a medically induced coma. The purpose of the medically induced coma is to allow the brain to rest. It also slows down the brain's electrical function. The coma keeps the brain from swelling and helps prevent other brain damage such as stroke or status epilepticus (Lewis, Sarah. 2020). Faber could not accept visitors except for immediate family members. Faber would never know he had visitors because he was in a coma; he was unconscious. Paramedics transported Sanders to the holding facility at Wishard Memorial Hospital. While at Wishard, Sanders was in the custody of the Marion County Sheriff. Doctors treated Sanders for the gunshot wounds he received from the police while at his residence. Sanders never left the holding facility until sometime later.

After the Dust Clears

While still at Fred Sanders' residence, Sergeant Sickels' plate was full. There was a mountain of work ahead of him, and the fun was getting started. The East District Field Captain stopped at the Sanders location to confer with Sickels regarding everything the Department required in a case of this magnitude. Detective Louis Christ, a homicide lieutenant, met with Sickels ensuring he was on the right track in completing the special departmental reports. The Lieutenant made sure Sickels had Faber's gun, holster, and identification and transported those items to the property branch. The Lieutenant wanted all officers' names and identification numbers at the Sanders scene, which Sickels could provide. Before he departed, the Lieutenant asks Sickels to report to the homicide branch for an interview later that evening.

Detective Lieutenant Louis Christ provided other information about Perry Evans, Sanders' neighbor across the street. Evans said he called the police because the dog was chasing his son, who escaped the dog by jumping on the hood of his car. Lieutenant Christ said Perry spoke to Matt when he first arrived. He told Matt about the dog chasing his son and jumping on top of his car. Evans told Lieutenant Christ, Faber crossed the street to talk with Fred Sanders. Evans said he saw them talking but did not hear what they said to each other. Evans said he saw Sanders turn around from Faber and started walking away. Evans stated Fred Sanders suddenly turned back towards Officer Faber, who appeared to stumble backward momentarily, then Faber started heading towards Sanders, who was going toward the front door. Maybe this was when Matt grabbed Sanders' shoulder, and Sanders turned around and shoved him. The conversation between Lieutenant Christ and Perry Evans occurred in front of Evans' house. Lieutenant Christ asked detective Sergeant Harry Dunn to get a formal statement from Perry Evans. But does not recall if the statement was taken from Perry's house or at police headquarters.

Before leaving the scene, Sergeant Sickels talks with officer Robert Ward. Ward had a cut to his left hand. Later it was discovered the wound needed three stitches. Ward said he was unsure how he cut his hand and did not notice the cut until it had been bleeding for a while. Ward told Sickels he and two other officers entered the back door of the house. They heard several gunshots, and all three fled through the back door. Sergeant Sickels told officer Ward to report to Wishard Memorial Hospital emergency room for treatment. Officers Marcus Kennedy and James Harris were the other officers entering the rear of the house. Neither of these officers stated anything different than what was already said by officer Ward. The scene was hectic and unpredictable.

There were too many officers on the scene. Most of them arrived at the shooting scene because they wanted to see what happened. Maybe they could catch a glimpse of Matt Faber. These officers had to be encouraged to leave the scene and go back to their patrol districts. Some came from as far away as the Northwest District, which is about six miles away. Those officers had no business leaving their District. An officer shot on duty does not happen often. It occurs about once every two and a half to four years. Fatalities occur around every five to seven years. Patrol officers are human and want to witness or see the activity happening. Sergeant Sickels has experienced six police officers killed on duty in twenty-seven years serving the Indianapolis Police Department.

Sergeant Sickels Leaves Sanders House

Sickels finally left the Sanders residence and headed to the Wishard Memorial Hospital emergency room. While at the hospital, the Sergeant needed to complete several of the special reports. While at the hospital, Sergeant Sickels completed an incident report of the events occurring at the Sanders home. He called in the report to the teletype section from the hospital. Twenty minutes later, the incident report became available department-wide. It took more than two hours for the Sergeant to complete these reports. When Sickels was ready to leave the hospital, patrol officers Fender and Ward had already left the emergency room. The emergency room doctors tended to their injuries, and they left. Emergency room doctors were treating Officer Faber for his gunshot wound. At that time, he was unconscious but later, the doctors induced him into a coma.

Leaving the hospital, Sergeant Sickels headed to police headquarters in downtown Indianapolis. He was en route to the Homicide Branch to see detective Lieutenant Louis Christ. He was going to take the statement from Sergeant Sickels. On arriving at police headquarters, Sergeant Sickels bumps into several officers inquiring about the status of Officer Faber. The entire Department is disappointed about what happened. Some officers are pleased to know a suspect was under arrest. Officers also expressed joy in knowing no other officer was injured. Sickels continued to the Homicide Branch. Upon reaching Homicide, it seemed as if you were in Union Station because the crowd of officers was so large. Sergeant Sickels had to wait fifteen minutes to see lieutenant Christ. The interview with Christ did not take long. The reason the interview was short is because Sergeant Sickels arrived late at Sanders' residence.

Sickels was not at Sanders' house when officers entered the front door or when the shooting occurred. Sickels never saw Sanders exit the front door or when handcuffs were chain-linked together behind his back to handcuff him. Sergeant Sickels could not give any new information regarding Sanders or shed new light on the case. Critical information for this case will come from officers or witnesses present during the initial front door entry. Or witnesses that were present while the shooting took place and the aftermath of the shooting. The aftermath includes when Fred Sanders exited the front door and handcuffs were placed on him while standing in the front yard. Sickels never witnessed any of these events occur at the Sanders house. Sickels would not make a good witness because he did not see anything that transpired during that time. What he did not see was of no importance or would have made any difference.

Sergeant Sickels left the Homicide Branch feeling a bit disappointed in his involvement in the Matt Faber case. Sickels began to believe during the critical stage at the Sanders home, he could have made a difference in what happened. Sickels had to make a stop at the Property Room to drop off some of Officer Faber's equipment. The equipment was his firearm, holster, ammunition, gun belt, nightstick, handcuffs, identification, badge, and hat. When an officer becomes injured on the job or incapacitated, the property room is typically responsible for holding departmental-issued equipment. The property room keeps detailed records of equipment it maintains. Everything brought to the property room is safe and not supposed to get lost.

The Three Dogs

The next day Sergeant Sickels and another officer went to Sanders' house to check on the dogs. The dogs did not appear to be in good health. Sanders' three dogs had a severe infestation of the dog mange. Mange refers to skin diseases caused by mites. The term comes from the French word mangue, which translates into 'to eat or itch.' A variety of mites can cause mange and affect many animals. Mange can affect humans too, which is commonly referred to as scabies. It's a common skin disease in dogs and puppies that are strays, neglected, or abused. If left untreated, this disease can cause serious health concerns, loss of skin, hair, lesions, and lacerations (Bovsun, Mara. January 23, 2019).

Fred Sanders' dogs appear to fit the description described above. These dogs did not have the proper care they needed. Sergeant Sickels asked to have Animal Control come to the Sanders residence. As Animal Control arrived at the Sanders residence, the officers said all three dogs have mange and is described as a severe case. All dogs appeared underfed, underweight, and skinny (Bovsun, Mara. January 23, 2019). The Catholic School principal said Fred was an animal lover and had brought a boa constrictor to school for the children to see. If Sanders was such a lover of animals, why didn't he properly care for his dogs? All of the dogs were in feeble physical health, it was apparent. Wonder what she would have thought if she had seen these dogs? The animal control officers confiscated the dogs, and they were taken to the dog pound. Most likely, the dog pound euthanized all of them.

Matt John Faber, Patrolman

Matthew John Faber was a twenty-four-year-old white police officer when Fred Sanders shot him. He was a patrol officer assigned to the late tactical shift of the East District. When Fred Sanders shot Matt, he had fourteen months of service to the Indianapolis Police Department. Matt was married to Jan Faber, an Indianapolis police officer assigned to the afternoon shift of the North District. They were married for just over two years. During Fred Sanders' shooting, Matt and Jan were legally separated and were well underway of divorce. At the time, Matt had a girlfriend who worked as a dispatcher for the Indianapolis Police Department. It was no secret, as many of Matt's friends knew of the relationship. They also were aware of the separation between Matt and Jan. Matt graduated from Indiana University with a degree in Physical Education. He was an exercise freak and loved working out. Matt told Sergeant Sickels, physical education was what attracted Jan and him together.

Although Sergeant Sickels was not Matt's direct supervisor, he knew him well. They would occasionally meet three or four times a week and have long discussions. Through these discussions, Sickels was beginning to understand Matt personally. One day, during a talk session, Matt told Sergeant Sickels he and Jan were legally separated and he now has a girlfriend. Matt told Sickels this occurred over the past six or seven weeks. Matt told Sickels he loved Jan but [sic] was not 'in love' with her. In a conversation, Matt said there were problems in their relationship that were impossible to repair. He felt separation was the best solution at that time. Faber wished there were no issues in their relationship. When they married, they were best friends and did everything together, including sharing an apartment. In another discussion with the Sergeant, Matt told Sickels he believed everything would work out as it should, and they would have a normal relationship.

The officers working with Matt, who was on his shift, liked him a lot. They considered him a friend and comrade and were willing to assist Matt on any run or assignment. Matt and his shift mates worked together well, like a well-oiled machine. This kind of relationship between shift members is typical and expected from officers in the Indianapolis Police Department. During the time Sickels knew Matt, the two went on numerous radio runs together. Sergeant Sickels' job as a supervisor is to ensure officers perform their duties according to department standards. Officers were required to comply with all rules and regulations, standard operating procedures, and departmental general orders. Officers must adhere to a ton of information called General Orders. All officers spend up to a year of training studying and complying with these procedures. Police Academy training is six months, followed by five months of field training.

During the five months of field training, all recruit trainees are evaluated daily. These evaluations can be grueling and repetitive. At times, recruit officers believe they are better than the evaluation results they are getting from their training officers. But to be smart about it, recruit officers must remain quiet and not rock the boat. Matt discussed this idea with Sergeant Sickels repeatedly. Matt talked and said [sic] 'there's good and bad in everything people do.' [sic] 'At times, we must bite the bullet.' For a young man, Matt was personable and made sense of life and living. Too bad he did not enjoy an entire life as he surely deserved that.

Fred Sanders

Fred Sanders was a forty-four-year-old white man who lived alone in an all- black neighborhood. On August 14, 1988, the day of the shooting, Fred was a Catholic school teacher. He taught at St. Luke Catholic School as a fourth- grade teacher in a northside neighborhood called Indian Hills over the last fourteen years. The location of Indian Hills is on the north side of Indianapolis. Neighbors have called the police on Fred Sanders in the past for various reasons. He was known to argue with neighbors and did so without any reason. He was known to have fired a gun at his neighbor across the street from his house. Neighbors complained about Fred's dogs running loose and chasing kids. Fred did little or nothing to alleviate these issues. The problems continued, and the neighborhood persisted in calling the police on Fred Sanders. Until August 14, 1988, Fred Sanders was somewhat of an unknown. He had no arrest record, and there was little or no information available about Fred Sanders.

His status as a Catholic school teacher was unknown immediately. It was seven to eight hours after the shooting Sanders' school teacher status leaked out. During the shooting, Fred Sanders was a huge man weighing more than two hundred and ninety pounds. He stood at five foot seven inches tall. You were wondering why it took two sets of handcuffs chain-linked together to handcuff him properly behind his back? In Indianapolis, all people arrested require behind-the-back handcuffing. Sanders was no exception to this rule. There are a few questions regarding Sanders' behavior; they are: Why did Sanders become so violent? Was there something special that triggered the violent behavior? Could violent behavior of this nature be prevented?

Something had to agitate Sanders to the point where he became unreasonable and angry toward Officer Faber. Behavior such as this was apparent because he would not listen or obey anything Officer Faber said, especially when Faber asked Fred Sanders to stop (walking). Fred Sanders knew Faber was a police officer because he saw him drive up in a police car, and Sanders asked Faber, "am I under arrest?" He knew Sergeant Knap and Officer Fender were police officers because they were wearing police uniforms. What possessed Sanders to resort to such ridiculous behavior and resort to using deadly force? Predicting violent behavior is a crapshoot, but sometimes someone gets it right. The best-trained psychologists and psychiatrists can't get this one right. They have to use their best guess as they may be right fifty percent of the time.

Sanders was not stupid and was a quick learner, especially after the shooting and when he was charged with shooting Officer Faber. He played on the sympathy of the news media and the public, in general. Early on, Sanders began to accuse the police of unnecessary force and brutality. He did this by making statements to the news media the police beat, hit, and kicked him. He told the news the abuse occurred while he was lying on the ground handcuffed. His comments were so intense they caused an internal affairs investigation of unnecessary force. These events laid the groundwork to begin his defense for the charge of murder.

Sanders carried this measure another step forward and played on the sympathy of the general public. St. Luke's Church members gathered in the courtroom where Fred was scheduled for a bail bond reduction hearing. When Sanders walked into the courtroom, the church members stood up and cheerfully applauded him. Several hundred church members gathered outside St. Luke's Church with protest signs who marched and chanted for the release of Fred Sanders. The local, news media documented these events in Indianapolis and caught the attention of Police Chief Paul Annee and the Indianapolis FOP (Fraternal Order of Police).

The Police Chief and FOP held their own news conferences admonishing the crowd in court and at St. Luke's Church protest. The Chief and FOP reiterated Fred Sanders murdered Matt Faber and should be held accountable for the offense. Later the church apologized for the behavior of church members stating they were only showing support, nothing else. A representative of the church said members' actions are out of context. Whatever the church stated, it was a cover-up from the truth. Church membership was interested in getting Sanders freed from arrest. They were united in this effort. Many members started a defense fund to help pay attorney fees for Sanders, believing he is innocent. These endeavors helped to embolden Sanders into thinking he was innocent of murder. Sanders honestly thought he was defending himself from the unlawful actions of a few Indianapolis police officers. In doing so, Sanders maintained his innocence throughout.

Fred Sanders was getting bolder as each day passed. He and his attorney were developing a defensive strategy against the murder charge. It even got worse for them because the Marion County Prosecutor added the death penalty sentence to the murder charge. Because of the death penalty, Sanders' attorney had to change his defense approach by delaying the court process. Sanders' attorney began filing several pre-trial motions. Some of these motions had to do with evidence and the criminal procedure. These motions only served to delay a trial, which was inevitable. What the attorney was doing was working for Sanders as time kept passing.

News of an internal affairs investigation about officers Fender and Ward began to leak out. Several weeks later, the news media announced both Fender and Ward were criminally charged for hitting Fred Sanders. A few days later, it was reported Robert Ward Jr. resigned from the Indianapolis Police Department and pleaded guilty to two charges of battery against Fred Sanders. The criminal charges against officers Fender and Ward resulted from the complaint made by Fred Sanders and the internal affairs investigation. It was sometime later, but Larry Fender's case was scheduled for trial in Marion County municipal court. During the process of the trial and procedures, the judge heard a motion by the defense counsel. After hearing the motion, the judge acquitted Fender of the criminal charges. For Fender, it was over. He was allowed to return to work and received back pay. As for Sanders, the outcome did not change their strategy.

Over time, Fred Sanders commented other officers assaulted him while he was being handcuffed and after he was handcuffed. Sanders accused specific officers of these assaults. One accusation he made accusing Sergeant Sickels of kicking him in the head. Sanders said, 'Sickels kicked me in the head like a football player was kicking a field goal.' He accused several officers of assaulting him in some fashion or other. The Indianapolis Police Department did not substantiate these accusations. Still, the news media kept a record of the allegations made by Sanders, and these accusations surfaced again, but it was much later. Sanders was thinking of a plan to use against the police department in his upcoming trial for murder. The truth of the matter was Sanders and his attorney had a strategy and took advantage of it on the trial date. The plan used by Sanders' attorney was grand and caught everyone by surprise.

Robert Ward Jr.

A Senseless Murder and the Indianapolis Police Department

Robert Ward Jr., a Patrolman, was a twenty-four-year-old man when he received an injury during the Fred Sanders shooting of Matt Faber. Robert served as a police officer for twenty-four months. Robert's father, Robert Ward Sr., served as the Deputy Chief of the Investigations Division. The Investigations Division is responsible for eighty percent of the Indianapolis Police Department's detectives and investigators. That would have been more than two hundred and fifty detectives. Ward's assignment was to the afternoon shift of the East District. At the time, the injury he sustained at Sanders' home was a bit confusing. Robert had a cut to his left hand and some fingers, for which he received treatment at Wishard Memorial Hospital. The hand injury required three stitches. Ward was later released on August 14, 1988, and dispatched to the Homicide Branch for an interview. After August 14, 1988, Sergeant Sickels never saw Robert Ward Jr. again. Information leaked out about two months later; there was an arrest of Ward relating to the Fred Sanders incident. The Department forced Robert Ward Jr. to resign from the Department. After leaving, Robert Ward took a job with the Indianapolis Airport Authority's fire department. He became a firefighter and worked there for several years.

A few weeks later, the word was out regarding Robert Ward and the battery arrest. He hit Fred Sanders several times while other officers were handcuffing him in the front yard. The cut to his hand and fingers were a result of his assault against Sanders. This information comes from the internal affairs investigation. Had Ward not resigned from the department, the Chief of Police would have moved to dismiss Ward for 'conduct unbecoming of an officer.' Ward could have appealed his decision, but he would be fighting an uphill and losing battle. He made the best choice considering the gravity of the matter. Without a doubt, it was a no-win and frustrating situation for Ward.

Larry Fender, Patrolman

Larry Fender, a Patrolman, was a thirty-two-year-old man when he received injuries during the Fred Sanders shooting of Matt Faber.

Larry served as a police officer for nine years. Fender's assignment was to the afternoon shift of the East District. Both of Larry's arms received abrasions, scrapes, and cuts. Larry Fender received treatment at Wishard Memorial Hospital and was released. Later in the evening, Larry was dispatched to the Homicide Branch to give a statement. Within five to six weeks after the Matt Faber shooting, Larry found himself at the Firearms Range doing menial worthless tasks. Fender found himself cutting the grass, picking up trash, cleaning the premises, and sometimes helping the range officers. He never asked for the reassignment. Fender completed his career working at the Firearms Range.

Over many years Sergeant Sickels would see Officer Fender at the Firearms Range. All Indianapolis police officers are required to qualify with their firearm(s) every 180 days or twice a year. All officers were assigned a sidearm which was a Glock firearms .30 caliber semi-automatic pistol. Uniformed officers would carry a seventeen-shot model, and detectives had an 11 shot model. During the early 2000s, the department began issuing long rifles to officers wanting them. Long rifle use was strictly voluntary but required specific training and qualifications. Rifle training was a five- day seminar. Officers qualifying with the rifle would be given one to carry in their car.

Sergeant Sickels would see Officer Fender during this time and noticed he was involved in training officers to use the rifle. Occasionally Sickels would engage Fender in conversation, but he never talked about the Matt Faber shooting, never. He did notice Fender helped in 'range scenarios,' he paid special attention while officers were doing their scenarios. The scenarios were designed to present officers with a 'real-time' live-action "shoot or don't shoot" situation. Each scenario had a pass/fail score. You passed if you shot during the scenario and failed if you didn't shoot. During the 2000s, Fender seemed to be satisfied with the range assignment.

Kent Knap, Sergeant

Kent Knap, a Sergeant, was a forty-seven-year-old white male. Kent was the first responder to the scene of the Matt Faber shooting. Kent served as an officer for more than twenty-five years, twelve of those years as a Sergeant. Sergeant Knap's assignment was to the late tactical shift of the East District. Kent was Faber's direct shift Sergeant. Kent responded quickly to Matt's call for assistance. Sergeant Knap was at Sanders' residence within minutes of Faber's call. Second to arrive was officer Larry Fender coming a few minutes later. Sergeant Knap remembers Faber telling him several things when he first arrived. Faber told Knap the man might have guns in the house. The man also was yelling obscenities and racial slurs to the neighbors in the area.

Kent Knap was the late tact shift sergeant and had been for several years. In the past, Knap told Sergeant Sickels he loved the tact shift hours as they fit his schedule perfectly. He said he prefers the late tact shift because he's tried all other shifts, and it works out better for him and his wife. Knap described working the shift gave him the freedom to do the things he needed to do daily and not be interrupted. He said every business is open during the time he is off. He can do almost anything he wants because he is not required to report for work until 7:00 p.m. Working from 7:00 p.m. to 3:00 a.m. goes fast, and the shift is over before you know it. Kent Knap worked his entire career in the Operations Division as a uniformed patrol officer and sergeant. He told Sergeant Sickels he never had an interest in being a detective or having a specialty job. He was satisfied with what he did and wanted to finish his career in uniform.

Sergeant Tommy Sickels

Sergeant Tommy Sickels was a thirty-five-year-old Japanese American (Mother Japanese – Father American) male Sergeant since 1986. Before the assignment to the East District, Sickels was an Accident Investigations relief sergeant for about a year. Before the East District assignment, Sickels was a Vice Branch Detective investigating gambling, prostitution, massage parlors, adult bookstores, illegal alcohol distribution, and dive joints (illegal bars).

Three years before Vice, Sickels was a detective investigating rape and child molesting in the Sex Crimes Branch.

Sergeant Sickels knew Knap reasonably well for several years before the Faber shooting occurred. Because they have overlapping shifts, the two would work together because the overlap was four hours each day. Over a few years, they would meet and have dinner with each other. Occasionally they would meet to discuss department events and issues. It was a good relationship. Kent Knap was a well-liked Sergeant and a good man. He knew the Department well and has seen almost everything a police officer or Sergeant could experience in less than a career's time. Kent Knap was senior as a supervisor to officers, and all supervisors or patrol officers could benefit from his experience.

A few years later, Sergeant Sickels transferred to another job in police headquarters. In the lobby of police headquarters, the two bumped into each other, where they engaged in conversation for several minutes. They have not seen each other for almost two years. Sickels noticed a large scar on Kent's neck. That is when Kent said he had throat cancer and had an operation. Because of the surgery, the surgeon removed his saliva gland. The absence of the saliva gland prevented saliva from secreting, which caused him to have a dry mouth. He was required to carry a squirt bottle and squirt water into his mouth to keep it moist constantly. During the conversation in police headquarters, Kent said he was cancer-free, and the police department had allowed him to resume work. He continued to work for many years after his bout with cancer.

Sergeant Sickels continued to work in police headquarters preventing him from occasionally meeting with friends from the police department, including Kent Knap. Except for the civil rights lawsuit brought on by Sanders in 1992, Sickels never saw Sergeant Knap again. It ended many years of friendship and camaraderie between the two. Sergeant Knap continued working as a field Sergeant but left the East District to work on the Northwest District. As for Sergeant Sickels, Kent Knap was larger than life. He meant a lot. However, his name and memories started to fade away through the passing years until they became distant memories.

Chapter Three
What Happens Next?

Since the Matt Faber shooting, the Department became very active regarding Fred Sanders and the shooting. The local media's accusations of police misconduct, excessive force, and conspiracies began to emerge. These stories were getting louder every day. Police misconduct and excessive force were the headline news for the newspapers and the local television news channels. At that time, the radio played a role in delivering news reports and was good at it. Every day after the Faber shooting for about two weeks, newspapers and television news outlets had to have stories about police brutality, police misconduct, or a coverup conspiracy regarding Fred Sanders' shooting. The stories and articles published about a conspiracy, police brutality, and coverup were baseless. Where did the news media outlets obtain their information to print or broadcast such nonsense? The information televised or published did not come from law enforcement or any of their associates. The Chief of Police, Paul Annee, was a solid supporter of the police department's members and what they stand for. As long as officers do not intentionally violate department rules and regulations, Chief Annee supported all officers, no matter the circumstances.

Chief of Police – Paul Annee

Paul Annee was an excellent Chief of Police for Indianapolis. Seven or eight days after the shooting, Chief of Police Paul Annee called for a news conference to reveal the facts of the investigation. The Chief laid all the information and facts on the table and allowed the news media to engage in a question-and-answer session. When the conference was over and the news media processed the information, they did not fully buy into the facts. They continued with their absurd approach that a conspiracy and a coverup theory existed by the supervisors of the police department. The news media did not let up on their belief, and they kept pushing for answers, which were obviously not there. They were entirely sure the police had something to hide, and they were going to find out what the secret is. What were they hiding? Chief Annee stated he did not care what the media said about the police department, but the murder of Matt Faber cannot go unnoticed when a police officer gets [sic] 'blown away' as Matt Faber did. The public cannot accept this type of behavior, regardless of who is pushing the narrative. If this becomes the case, our nation will end up in anarchy (Morgan, August 25, 1988).

Matt Faber's Condition

Matt Faber dies nine days after Fred Sanders shot him with a .12-gauge shotgun at almost 'point-blank' range. That's very close. On Tuesday, August 22, 1988, Matt Faber died at Wishard Memorial Hospital at about 7:30 p.m. while in the intensive care unit. In a newspaper clipping, Sergeant Sickels cut from the *Indianapolis Star* dated August 22, 1988, he made the following comment. 'Everyone's pretty saddened by what's happened,' said Sergeant Sickels, one of Faber's supervisors on the night shift. 'Everyone wants to be a little more careful tonight. They're going to be sticking together.' While being treated for the gunshot wound in Wishard Memorial Hospital on Tuesday afternoon, an infection began to cause Matt Faber's condition to decline. This condition came on quickly and caught the doctors by surprise. By the time they began working on him, there was no chance of his survival. Hospital officials said the wound was massive, caused by a .12-gauge shotgun blast (*Indianapolis Star*, August 22, 1988). Incidentally, Sergeant Sickels was the night shift Sergeant, and Officer Faber was on the late-tactical shift.

The day before Faber's death was Wednesday, August 21, 1988. A bond reduction hearing was to take place in Criminal Court Six. The prosecutor intended to charge Sanders with murder and file for the death penalty. These were the words coming from

A Senseless Murder and the Indianapolis Police Department

the mouth of Marion County Prosecutor Stephen Goldsmith, who was nearing the end of his second term in office. Goldsmith's second term ended December 31, 1991. He ran for the Mayor of Indianapolis, and he won the race, taking office on January 1, 1992. The same Wednesday morning in Criminal Court Six, the bond reduction hearing would occur in the early a.m. As Sanders appeared in the courtroom, a group of almost one hundred St. Luke School parishioners was in the same courtroom. The parishioners stood up and applauded Sanders in a show of support while he walked into the courtroom. How disgusting can this get, celebrating a murderer? What is happening to the world? Is this the direction our world is heading? Murder a cop and get an award.

Because the parishioners disrupted the court proceedings, the judge postponed the bond hearing indefinitely. During the same day, around 9:00 a.m., almost 200 parishioners held a rally outside St. Luke's School, showing their support for Fred Sanders. These parishioners were carrying signs and chanting support slogans throughout the protest. The Indianapolis police responded by criticizing the school; hooray for the *Indianapolis Star* newspaper. The attending parishioners say what they did is shameful and glorified Sanders for murdering a police officer. They should have mourned Officer Faber's death. Instead, these people riled up the entire law enforcement community and Faber's family in an attempt to shame and disgrace them. At that time, these kinds of activities were unheard of and would never occur. In this case, it happened—what a shame.

Funeral

Three days later, the police department conducted the funeral for officer Matt Faber. The funeral took place in two locations. 1) The Feeney-Hornak Westgate Mortuary 2) The burial site for Matt was in Floral Park Cemetery.

Today it has been renamed as West Ridge Park Cemetery 9295 West 21st Street. Both sites were on the far west side of Indianapolis.

The date of the funeral was Friday, August 25, 1988. The burial site was very close to the Mortuary, just a short drive away. More than five hundred people turned out to show their respect for Officer Faber. The Feeney-Hornak Westgate Mortuary was too small to accommodate all of the mourners. More than three hundred mourners gathered outside the Mortuary and listened to the funeral services through a loudspeaker. Chief of Police Paul Annee gave the eulogy during the service, while several other guest speakers shared their heartfelt memories of Officer Faber. An overflow crowd of mourners gathered around a loudspeaker in the mortuary's parking lot to listen as Police Chief Paul A. Annee remembered 'his smiles, his sense of humor, his ability to lift a friend's spirits at the end of the day.' Police officers across America and numerous officers from Indiana came to join and celebrate Matt's funeral. There were police officers from many states as the markings on their police cars would identify them. The show of solidarity and strength was overwhelming because many people and officers attended the funeral.

A Senseless Murder and the Indianapolis Police Department

(*Indianapolis Star*. Friday, August 25, 1988)

It is a tradition for the Indianapolis Police Department to respect fallen officers from the Department. The mayor orders the flags to be flown at half-staff for a few days in all cases of a fallen officer of the Indianapolis Police Department. All police officers in Indianapolis and Marion County, Indiana, will wear a black band around the middle of their badge for a week. The Police Chaplin's Office will prepare the funeral arrangements. The Police Chaplin's Office has a staff of five Chaplin's and a Head Chaplin. Police funerals draw a lot of attention from the news media, newspapers, local television and radio news broadcasts, and the community. The news media gets their chance of taking their best photographs. Broadcasters will put their best foot forward during their programs. The funeral will be the biggest story that day. They will attempt to capture how large the crowd appears inside and outside the funeral home and when the casket 'rolls by' police headquarters. Newspapers will make close-up photographs of dignitaries and family members to be included in future stories. The entire display of the funeral is big news, and local news media will not miss this for a second.

Other Indianapolis Police Officers Die in Line of Duty

Before Matt Faber's murder, Jack Ohrberg was the last Indianapolis police officer murdered. The murder occurred in late December 1980 while Jack Ohrberg was serving an arrest warrant on Tommy Smith. Smith was wanted for murder and other related charges. Tommy Smith used a machine gun and fired through the front door where he was staying while Ohrberg knocked on the door. There have been several officers killed on duty, but they died in motor vehicle accidents. One was Sergeant David Sandler, who died in a police motorcycle crash. A driver pulled in front of him at an intersection, failing to yield the right of way. Sergeant David Sandler was not able to stop and died on impact.

While fleeing from the police in his car, a criminal intentionally hit head- on the police car coming in the opposite direction on Holt Road. Officer Paul A. Kortepeter, who was driving the police car, was killed instantly from the impact. The motor vehicle crash occurred on January 19, 1983. The three police officer deaths were all accompanied by large funerals and a show of camaraderie. In the history of the Indianapolis Police Department, more than sixty police officers lost their lives working as Indianapolis Police Officers. At the time of their deaths, these officers were on duty. Many of them were murdered or intentionally killed. Others died from accidents or other tragedies. In all cases of on-duty deaths, a funeral follows. These funerals are large and attended by hundreds of law enforcement personnel all across the United States. The funeral process allows the police department, officers and supervisors, community and family members, and special interest groups to witness and respect what their loss means to the community. People just don't poke fun at murdered police officers. Instead, they should show respect. In this case, these things did not happen in the Matt Faber murder and funeral.

(Photo: Indianapolis Police Department, 1984)

Patrol Officer Teresa Jean Hawkins, twenty-eight, died in a pre-dawn automobile accident on Tuesday, August 17, 1993, while assisting an ambulance crew with a patient at 38th Street and Emerson Avenue. As she drove on Emerson, with red and blue lights flashing, a 1978 Ford LTD driven by Elvis L. Lacy ran a stop sign at Emerson and 36th Street.

Lacy was driving over the 30 M.P.H. posted speed limit. He had a blood-alcohol level of 0.191 percent, almost twice the legal standard for intoxication. The Ford struck the driver's door of Officer Hawkins' Chevrolet Caprice, pushing the squad car into a utility pole. Lacy was charged with reckless homicide, operating a motor vehicle while intoxicated, causing death, and driving with a blood-alcohol content over the legal limit, causing a death.

All three charges were class C felonies, calling for a maximum sentence of eight years. However, because all three charges were based on the same facts, only one penalty of eight years could be imposed. Lacy pled guilty and received a maximum of eight years in prison.

A 1983 graduate of Tipton High School and a 1987 graduate of Ball State University, Officer Hawkins' ambition to go into law enforcement began when she babysat for the three children of a Tipton County deputy sheriff.

Hundreds of police officers from Michigan, Kentucky, and throughout Indiana attended services for Officer Hawkins. Patrol Officer Anna Bies, a friend, and co-worker stood before the nine hundred mourners and gave an emotional and moving eulogy as told those assembled:

Fifty-seven officers and two canines lost their lives while on duty for the Indianapolis Police Department. The Department keeps and maintains records on these officers and the events that led to their deaths. In 2007 the Indianapolis Police Department was legally dissolved and replaced by the Indianapolis Metropolitan Police Department. Since that date, four officers have been murdered while working on duty. The Chaplin's Office keeps and maintains these records. They also keep a large display of memorabilia of these officers for the public to view in the Chief of Police Office.

Regarding Fred Sanders, the community and people's involvement became twisted and distorted from the facts of the Matt Faber shooting. Is it like comparing the Fred Sanders shooting to the resistance movement of the Vietnam War? People were fighting against the war, saying it was wrong and inhumane as they did in the Fred Sanders shooting. These people wanted to show their support and resistance to what was happening because they had a cause, or they thought. In Fred Sanders, the reality of what was happening did not add up. It wasn't making sense, and they did not have a legitimate reason to protest. They were chasing an elusive or imaginary dream that should not survive. The same events occurred during the Vietnam War, but it got much more violent during that time.

CHAPTER FOUR
Fred Sanders and the Indianapolis Criminal Courts

Newspaper Article

You can read from Figure 6, Indianapolis Police Department Arrest Report Form. Fred Sanders had several charges placed against him. They were 1) Attempted murder, 2) resisting arrest with a deadly weapon causing serious bodily injury, 3) battery on a police officer with injury. These criminal charges are felony crimes punishable by more than a year in jail or prison if pleading or found guilty in a court of law. While in Indiana, the term "attempt" is when a defendant makes a substantial step toward carrying out any crime but fails to complete the crime. Officers will arrest a defendant charging them with an attempt, and list the crime they attempted to commit. Punishment for attempted crimes carries the same penalty as if the defendant completed carrying out the complete crime. Attempted crimes can be a felony which are crimes punishable for more than one year in jail or prison, or they can be misdemeanor crimes that can be punishable for up to one year, but not more than a year in jail. Attempt statutes began to show up in the Indiana Criminal Code in the early to middle seventies. Since that time, police officers in Indiana have enjoyed using attempt charges. The ability to use the attempt statutes allows law enforcement officers to make arrests before they couldn't. Before attempt charges were available, officers had to let offenders free.

(*Indianapolis Star*. August 24, 1988)

Criminal Charges – Officer Robert Ward and Officer Larry Fender

As the case is proceeding through the courts in Indianapolis, Sanders' defense attorney objects to everything the Indianapolis prosecutors are doing or attempted to do with the incident. Fred began making accusations the police used excessive force against him during and after his arrest. He continued these complaints until such time the Department began to take a look at them. The internal affairs branch investigated Sanders' complaint of unnecessary force. Their findings were never published anywhere or by anybody. Prosecutors charged Larry Fender with a crime relating to the internal affairs investigation. He was arrested on two counts of battery with injury against Fred

Sanders. In a trial in December 1990, a judge acquitted Larry Fender on the criminal charges against him (O'Neil, November 19, 1992).

Earlier it was unclear whether the prosecutor brought criminal charges against Robert Ward. But later, it was revealed criminal charges against Robert Ward demonstrated that in 1990, he pleaded guilty to the criminal charges relating to the Fred Sanders event. Shortly after the guilty plea Robert Ward resigned from the Indianapolis Police Department. City Attorney Joseph Perkins said, 'the city is not required to pay any judgment awarded to Ward for criminal acts. This issue needs to be discussed before the question can be answered' (O'Neil, November 24, 1992). Robert Ward disappeared from the police department. Rumors began to spread Ward was forced to resign against his will, and someone within the Department coerced him into signing his resignation. In the meantime, Fred Sanders filed a civil rights lawsuit against the police department for police brutality and excessive force.

Indiana Supreme Court Upholds Sanders Lower Court Conviction

Initially, Fred Sanders pleaded guilty to involuntary manslaughter in a Marion County criminal court. He was sentenced to seven years in prison. What happened to the charges of murder with death penalty charges? However, later Sanders disputed his guilty plea. Saying the Court did not adequately advise him of the guilty plea. Initially, the State charged Sanders with two counts of attempted murder. The prosecutor added a second charge of resisting law enforcement, resulting in bodily injury. Later the State dismissed the death penalty murder charge. The State proceeded with the other criminal charges. Before the trial on January 31, 1989, Sanders pleaded guilty to involuntary manslaughter. The reason for the plea will dismiss all additional criminal charges against Sanders. The Court and Sanders agreed to this plea agreement. In reality, Sanders never was officially charged with the criminal charge of involuntary manslaughter. However, he pleads guilty to this charge as a lesser-included offense of murder. In Indiana, anyone found or pleads guilty to felony crimes must have a pre-sentence investigation conducted before a judge can sentence them. After the pre-sentence investigation, the Court sentenced Sanders to seven years (Supreme Court of Indiana. 596 N.E.2d 225, July 20, 1992).

'The real problem of this case is mentioned in the petition and becomes the heart or root issue for Fred Sanders.' The crux of the problem presented in this case is that the verified petition was admitted into evidence for a limited purpose and was specifically not being admitted into evidence for the truth of the matters contained within the petition. After admitting the petition into evidence with the understanding that it was not being admitted for the truth of the matters contained within the petition, the trial court erroneously considered the petition as if the petition had been admitted into evidence to prove the truth of the allegations contained therein. The Court of Appeals affirmed the trial court's judgment by committing the same error relying on the evidence admitted for a limited purpose and not for the truthfulness of the facts alleged in order to support findings of fact. 'Both the trial and appellate courts were incorrect in utilizing the petition in this manner' (Supreme Court of Indiana. 596 N.E.2d 225, July 20, 1992).

Sanders did not prove his case in the Appeals Court, and the Supreme Court agreed. This is what the Supreme Court said about Sanders. 'The prejudice to the State is apparent. Because the Sanders petition was not being admitted for the truth of the allegations recited in the petition, the State did not cross-examine Sanders or call Sanders' trial counsel in an attempt to refute or impeach the facts alleged in the petition. A new hearing on Sanders' petition for post-conviction relief would be required to allow the State the opportunity to rebut the claims made by Sanders in his petition. The State, however, argues that absent the allegations of fact contained in the petition, the evidence is insufficient to establish that Sanders' guilty plea was not knowing, voluntary, or intelligent. Therefore, the State urges that he failed to prove his case, and his petition must be denied. We agree. When Sanders pled guilty to involuntary manslaughter, he was pleading guilty to a lesser-included offense of the crime of murder. No separate information or indictment was necessary in order to put

Sanders on notice of the charges' (Supreme Court of Indiana. 596 N.E.2d 225, July 20, 1992).

The final comments of the Supreme Court clarified that Sanders had a good understanding of the charges and his plea agreement with the State and the Court. His plea satisfies the Constitutional requirement set forth by prior case law. 'The evidence is undisputed that hearing, the State read the statutory definition of involuntary Manslaughter to Sanders during the guilty plea.' Also, the probable cause affidavit previously filed in the case was read to Sanders. This affidavit set out in detail the facts surrounding the killing. Following the reading of the statute and probable cause affidavit, Sanders was then asked specifically if he was pleading guilty to the crime charged. He replied in the affirmative. Additionally, when asked why he felt he was guilty of involuntary manslaughter, Sanders demonstrated an understanding of the nature of the charge when he answered that he recklessly pointed a shotgun at Faber (Supreme Court of Indiana. 596 N.E.2d 225, July 20, 1992).

This undisputed evidence from the transcript of the guilty plea hearing satisfies the constitutional requirement set forth in Henderson v. Morgan (1976). Sanders was aware of the elements of the offense of involuntary manslaughter when he pled guilty. Absent his verified petition, which was admitted not for the truth of the matters stated, but merely to set forth the allegations of his claim, there is not sufficient evidence to support the trial judge's determination that his plea was not knowingly, voluntarily, and intelligently entered. Thus, 'the trial court's findings of fact were clearly erroneous and must be set aside. And, without those findings of fact, the judgment granting Sanders' petition must be reversed and remanded to the trial court with instructions to deny the petition. Accordingly, we grant the State's Petition to Transfer, vacate the opinion of the Court of Appeals, reverse the trial court and remand this matter to the trial court to deny the petition for post-conviction relief charges' (Supreme Court of Indiana. 596 N.E.2d 225, July 20, 1992).

An Indiana Supreme Court brief filed February 27, 1992, states the following from the Indiana Court of Appeals. 'The State of Indiana appeals from an order granting Fred C. Sanders' petition for post-conviction relief.' Sanders pled guilty to involuntary manslaughter for killing a police officer by shooting him in the back with a shotgun. 'He was sentenced to seven (7) years imprisonment. Sanders convinced the post-conviction Court that his guilty plea was not entered knowingly, voluntarily, and intelligently because he had not received real notice of the true nature of the crime of involuntary manslaughter and was under the mistaken impression that self-defense was not available as a defense to involuntary manslaughter. We affirm' (Supreme Court of Indiana. 587 N.E.2d 166, February 27, 1992).

As reviewed by the Indiana Supreme Court, the Justices did not buy into Sanders' appeal and rejected it on its face, basically saying they did not believe him. Throughout the brief were statements Owen Mullin, attorney for Fred Sanders, included in the Appellate Court brief. The comments of Mr. Sanders are essential because they will demonstrate Sanders' demeanor through this appeals process. 'At the guilty plea hearing, the statute defining involuntary manslaughter was read into the court record as follows.'

'According to Indiana Code 35-42-1-4, entitled "Involuntary Manslaughter," A person who kills another human being while committing or attempting to commit (1) a Class C or Class D Felony that inherently poses a risk of serious bodily injury; (2) a Class A Misdemeanor that inherently poses a risk of serious bodily injury; or (3) battery, commits involuntary manslaughter, a Class C Felony. However, if the killing results from the operation of a vehicle, the offense is a Class D Felony' (Supreme Court of Indiana. 587 N.E.2d 166, February 27, 1992).

'Sanders indicated he was guilty of involuntary manslaughter by stating, "Judge, I recklessly pointed a shotgun at an officer." On October 24, 1990, Sanders filed a petition for post-conviction relief, which contains the following. 1) State concisely all the grounds known to you for vacating, setting aside, or correcting your conviction and sentence? 2) The Petitioner did not knowingly, voluntarily, and intelligently enter a plea of guilty in this cause to the crime of involuntary manslaughter. 3) State concisely and in the same order the facts which support each of the grounds set forth.' In a rather lengthy and elongated response, Sanders replies in total (Supreme Court of Indiana. 587 N.E.2d 166, February 27, 1992).

'At the time of my guilty plea in this Court on January 31, 1989, neither the State of Indiana, the Court, nor my counsel, furnished me in writing or read to me an information setting out the crime to which I was pleading guilty.' In particular, the underlying crime, which must be the basis of the crime of involuntary manslaughter, was not set out. 'Neither the State of Indiana, the Court, nor my counsel informed me the (sic) necessary elements for any such underlying crime. The only thing the State did, when asked by the judge to read me the information,' was read the Indiana Code, § 35-42-1-4 entitled, 'Involuntary Manslaughter.' See pages 4 and 5 of the Transcript of Guilty Plea attached hereto as 'Exhibit A.' Sanders said, 'The Court then asked me if I understood the information, and I said, "yes," but there was no information, and I did not understand. The Court then asked me if I understood that I was pleading guilty to and admitting as true everything that Mr. Cook, the Chief Deputy Prosecutor, had alleged, which I said, "yes" but there was nothing alleged, nor an information read nor facts given, and I did not understand.' See page 5 of Exhibit A. 'From the time of the incident on August 14, 1988, until the present, I have told everyone that I was being beaten and acted in self-defense. I said this to Officer Bastian, who was the first police officer who interviewed me at the hospital that night. I have never deviated, nor will I ever deviate from this truth: I acted in self-defense. My counsel advised me that this was an absolute defense, and I would not be convicted of murder' (Supreme Court of Indiana. 587 N.E.2d 166, February 27, 1992).

August 14, 1988 was a steaming hot day. Perry Evans summons the police to his house because Sanders' dog chased one of his (Perry's) kids while the child was riding a scooter. Perry explained why he called the police on the complaint. Based on the facts of the complaint, the officer would be limited in what action he could or could not take in this matter. The standard procedure that Indianapolis police officers take starts out with a discussion. Usually, officers jot information in their field notebooks in case they need it for a report. In reality, this is what Officer Faber was attempting to do. Faber approached Fred Sanders, standing near the sidewalk in his front yard, just across the street from Perry Evans' house. Officer Faber approaches Sanders and asks him about his dogs. Sanders interrupts

Faber by asking, 'Am I under arrest?' Faber replied, 'no.' At that time, Fred Sanders turned around and walked toward the front door. Is this what a reasonable person would do in a case such as this? Fred should have continued the conversation with Officer Faber. The incident would have ended peacefully with Faber leaving the scene and Sanders going back into his house. The majority of the police calls for service end in this manner. Officer Faber would have checked back in-service without a report. By using police jargon, it's called '10-8 (in-service) no report.'

Unfortunately, the latter did not happen, and the entire community had to deal with a double tragedy. Action taken by Sanders created a chain link of events that started the day of the shooting. In all, nearly sixty police officers responded in some manner to the Faber call for assistance. Numerous officers did not stay at the Sanders residence. They would drive up to the scene, look around and leave. Many of them did not get out of their patrol cars and would drive off.

During Sanders' criminal charges of murder, he and his attorney made numerous pre-trial hearings. It appeared (matter of expression) as if they were in a pre-trial hearing every week. They used every angle they could throw at the city of Indianapolis to thwart the murder charges. These maneuvers took time, patience, and money, but they were gaining ground in their efforts. Sanders' criminal attorney, Owen Mullins, was successful in the actions he was taking. He carefully prepared for the murder charge. He did everything the right way to get what he wanted from the Marion County prosecutors. David Cook, the Chief Deputy Prosecutor, was calling all the shots for the Marion County Prosecutor's Office. He was making all of the decisions at that time. Even though David Cook was calling the shots, Stephen Goldsmith was the elected prosecutor of Marion County. He is the final decision maker; Goldsmith had to approve agreements David Cook made.

The decision by the Indiana Supreme Court shed new light on the Sanders case. It offered a breath of fresh air that would help change the direction of the case. The Court's decision was necessary because Sanders' case was becoming stagnant. Fred Sanders' case was headed to nowheresville, and fast. The Indiana Supreme Court mandated the case back to the original Court of jurisdiction for a new trial. However, the Sanders legal team sat on it and did nothing. Although the case was sent back to the original court, it never was retried. Sometime in 1991, Sanders left jail indefinitely on a bond of one hundred thousand dollars. The release had to do with his attorney filing an appeal of his guilty plea. In his post-conviction petition, Sanders says the Court nor his attorney correctly represented him. Neither the Court nor his attorney furnished Sanders in writing or reading any form of information setting out the crime or specifying the specifics his guilty plea entailed. How could Sanders and his attorney get by with this nonsense? Maybe it's not understood clearly if a case is mandated back to an original trial court of jurisdiction by a Supreme Court, can the defense attorney simply sit on the case and do nothing? What would be the purpose of appealing a court case to an Appeals or Supreme Court?

Indiana Supreme Court Rejects Sanders Post-Conviction Relief

Let's put the Indiana Supreme Court's decision in the proper perspective. The Court rejects Sanders' motion for post-conviction relief and sends the trial back to the original Court in Indianapolis. He is freed on a hundred thousand dollars bond and never has the case retried. He spends less than three years in jail for his original plea bargain deal. However, his sentence was for a seven-year term in Indiana a person serves half the jail time. Sanders would be required to spend half of the seven-year sentence, which would have been three and a half years. He did not complete his sentence and was released after spending less than three years. He needed to be in jail for more than six more months.

The early release came under scrutiny by then Marion County Prosecutor Jeffrey Modisett. On December 11, 1992, Prosecutor Modisett filed a motion for the State of Indiana v Fred Sanders to have Sanders immediately serve out the rest of his jail sentence. Modisett's theory is as follows. The assumption is that the United States Supreme Court will review Sanders' case. In such a review, there must be a Constitutional question. The Indiana Supreme Court ruled the defense did not have sufficient evidence in support of post-conviction relief. According to Modisett, this is hardly an issue of Constitutional dimensions (Smith, December 11, 1992). Sanders never completed serving his sentence. Sanders' attorney never refiled his original trial in Marion County. Marion County Prosecutors sent a letter to the trial court to deny Sanders' request for post-conviction relief. Where is justice in all this madness? What was the purpose of Sanders' appeal?

Sanders filed a petition for post-conviction relief on October 24, 1990. The Court verifies the authenticity of the petition. The petition says, as quoted by Sanders, the following 'neither the State of Indiana, the Court, nor my counsel, furnished me in writing or read to me an information setting out the crime to which I was pleading guilty.' Additional comments, Sanders declares that 'neither the State of Indiana, the Court, nor my counsel, informed me the [sic] necessary elements for any such underlying crime.' Reading from the Indiana Supreme Court transcript, it becomes astounding to believe Sanders' attorney would write such nonsense. The content of the writing amazes anybody reading this garbage.

As cited directly from the transcript, Sanders' attorney told him to enter the guilty plea because his counsel was not ready to try the murder charge. His attorney told him, 'you are, in fact, guilty of involuntary manslaughter in that you had acted recklessly in causing the death of Faber.' Furthermore, the petition alleges Sanders was 'never advised of the legal definition of "reckless" or "recklessly" and that had he been so advised, he would not have pleaded guilty.' During the hearing, the counsel for Sanders stated his theory to the Court. He said, 'the guilty plea should be set aside because, at the time of the guilty plea hearing, there was no charging document (either information or indictment) that charged Sanders with involuntary manslaughter.' Sanders' legal premise was that, as a matter of law, a defendant could not knowingly enter into a guilty plea to the charge of involuntary manslaughter unless an information or indictment is charging him with the crime of involuntary manslaughter (Supreme Court of Indiana. 596 N.E.2d 225, July 20, 1992).

A Senseless Murder and the Indianapolis Police Department

Indianapolis police officers could not believe what occurred to the Fred Sanders arrest. All officers thought he would be facing Capital Murder charges because Sanders murdered a police officer. Police Chief Paul Annee publicly supported the death penalty for Fred Sanders. So did the prosecutor, Steve Goldsmith. Capital murder triggers the death penalty to be available if a defendant is found guilty. In many capital offenses, the death penalty becomes a reality. When a person is found guilty of a capital offense and receives a death sentence, it takes many years to carry out the penalty phase. It can take from ten to twenty-one years for the execution to take place. It takes a long time because the appeals process must be allowed to take place properly. Allowing all avenues of redress must be permitted to be a thousand percent correct. It's better to be safe than to be sorry. In the Police Academy, officers learn the differences between murder and involuntary manslaughter. Initially, Marion County Prosecutor Stephen Goldsmith asserted to file the death penalty charges against Fred Sanders. Indianapolis police officers looked forward to watching Fred Sanders going to court and facing the death penalty. The death penalty would have been appropriate justice.

Little did anyone know the next play in the playbook was ground-shaking. The community would have been shocked. Had this been the known play, someone should have tripped Sanders, causing him to fall fifteen flights of stairs to his death. As opposed to having all of this nonsense occur, what a disappointment for everyone interested in seeing something positive happen. Again, back to Fred Sanders and his ability to escape justice. Regardless of whether Robert Ward and Larry Fender faced charges of assaulting Fred Sanders. The prosecutor should never have agreed to such nonsense. Sanders was guilty of murder that deserved the death penalty, nothing less. What he got was a crystal palace lined with gold begging him to sue the Indianapolis Police Department and strip it from its pedestal. A thorough slap in the face and no apologies. A reward for murdering one of Indianapolis' Finest. How can there be such injustice in a just society? What a shame!

Stephen Goldsmith served two terms as Mayor of Indianapolis from 1992 to 2000, and he replaced Bill Hudnut as mayor. Goldsmith was not Mayor when Fred Sanders murdered Matt Faber. William

(Bill) Hudnut was Mayor from 1976 to 1992, replacing Dick Lugar. Goldsmith was Marion County prosecutor for twelve years serving from 1979 to 1991. Goldsmith stated publicly several times he was pushing for the death penalty of Sanders. He was the prosecutor when Fred Sanders murdered Matt Faber. Paul Annee was the Chief of Police. Chief Paul Annee stated publicly that the prosecutor needs to ensure the death penalty will follow. Chief Annee reinforced this statement publically several times. Annee said the Department took too many steps backward because of what occurred. These ideas or suggestions got the support of the public, but the idea never got off the ground. Jeffrey Modisett was Marion County Prosecutor for four years, 1991 to 1994. However, Stephen Goldsmith was the Marion County Prosecutor when Fred Sanders pleaded guilty to involuntary manslaughter. On January 31, 1989, Fred Sanders made the guilty plea. You put the puzzle together. Who was involved in the plea agreement with the County Prosecutors and Fred Sanders' attorney?

It's easy to rule out Chief Paul Annee. He is a die-hard police officer all the way through and wants proper justice to occur. Nothing less would be acceptable for the senseless murder of a young police officer. Because the plea agreement occurred on January 31, 1989, Jeff Modisett was not Marion County Prosecutor. It's easy to rule him out too. Mayor Hudnut and prosecutor Stephen Goldsmith are the leftovers along with Sanders' attorney. However, it is unlikely that Mayor Hudnut would get involved in plea negotiations with any court, prosecutor, or defense attorney. Logically and practically, it leaves the prosecutor, Goldsmith, and the defense attorney. These were the only two left. Who else can it be? Think about it. Goldsmith is eyeing the mayor's office in a year. He doesn't need a blemish on his political record to stand in his way. It makes sense because it's politics. Here are a few considerations to think about in connection to the plea agreement. The news media did not get a heads up of the plea agreement. That would have been big news. Somehow, it was kept quiet or done secretly. Someone had something to gain from the plea agreement, which usually translates into three things 1) money, 2) promises, and 3) power. So, where does the cookie crumble?

Before or around January 31, 1989, the news media, newspapers, radio, and television news never discussed or printed a plea agreement deal. The prosecutor's office and Fred Sanders' attorney kept the plea agreement under the radar. It was a big secret hidden from everyone. When the parties signed off on the plea agreement in Criminal Court that morning, the news media caught wind of the plea agreement and had a heyday. Local television stations broadcast the plea agreement story on the 6:00 p.m. and 11:00 p.m. The *Indianapolis Star* and Marion County local newspaper outlets printed the feature story the following day. Would you please take a look at what happened to Goldsmith after he left as Indianapolis Mayor? He became a deputy mayor of New York City. In less than a year, he began failing in that job and had to resign from embarrassment. Later that year, his wife divorced him. He was falling apart. What happened to this man? He was on his way to political stardom but crashed.

Why was the information kept secret? In terms of the Fred Sanders case, this would have been big news. The opportunity to experience this news event was crucial, but it never occurred. The prosecutor's office had to be the plan's architect to keep the plea agreement hidden from the public and the police department. These will not be the facts, according to Sanders and his attorney. Sanders' attorney at the time was Owen Mullin, who told Sanders he was not ready to try the case. Mullin said he was not prepared. Mullin told Sanders in January of 1989. He arranged for him to plead guilty to involuntary manslaughter. Sanders told Mullin he was guilty of involuntary manslaughter. Sanders went further and said, "I had acted recklessly. I understood, as a layman, 'reckless' to mean lack of proper caution or careless. I defended myself from the assault of the police. My counsel advised me that what I did was carelessness, and I was, thus, guilty of involuntary manslaughter." Sanders further said, 'Had I been advised by my counsel, the Court, or the prosecutor this was the underlying element of the crime, I would never have pleaded guilty' (Supreme Court of Indiana 587 N.E.2d 166, February 27, 1992).

It appears Sanders' attorney, Owen Mullin, had struck an agreement with Marion County prosecutors to allow him to plead guilty to involuntary manslaughter. The author stumbled across this brief filed by the Court that contained a wealth of information. The brief explains a lot of what Sanders thought of while he was waiting. If you were to read the brief thoroughly, you would believe Sanders has a severe mental case. How could a guy like him be a teacher? Let alone a Catholic fourth-grade teacher who was supposed to have a good reputation with the school. It is essential readers can read some of the comments made by Fred Sanders. The statements made by Sanders will adequately set the stage for his behavior, demeanor, and attitude regarding the police in general. But what Sanders thought of the police when they came to his house on the dog complaint is surprising. Nothing ever describes his dogs that neighbors constantly complained of misbehaving. By the time the police arrived at Sanders' home, the dogs were in their pen. Have you ever heard the term 'mangy mutts?' Those were the dogs kept in Sanders' dog pin; those were Fred's dogs with the mange. Fred, the animal lover.

CHAPTER FIVE
Civil Rights Lawsuit. U.S. District Court, Indianapolis

The Trial Phase

Owen Mullin was the attorney for the Sanders Marion County Criminal Court case. Douglas Shortridge was the attorney for Sanders' Civil Rights lawsuit. The United States Southern District Court has the jurisdiction of this lawsuit. The court is in downtown Indianapolis, Indiana. The court has jurisdiction in Federal civil rights lawsuits and Federal Criminal cases for the Southern District of Indiana. In 1992, the presiding judge was Sarah Evans Barker, an experienced federal judge. In the United States, there are ninety-two federal district courts. At a minimum, there is one court in every state, but some states have more than one district. There are districts in several countries such as Puerto Rico, the Virgin Islands, Guam, and the Northern Mariana Islands. District courts have exclusive jurisdiction in all bankruptcy cases in the United States.

In addition to the district court judges, magistrate judges in almost all districts assist in preparing cases for trial. These judges will conduct trials at the district level for misdemeanor criminal cases. All United States federal judges are appointed by the President and serve a lifetime appointment. Once an appointment as a federal judge, the job is fairly protected in security and tenure. Most of these judges stay until age prevents them from performing their duties. Today the pay for a U.S. District judge is 229,000 dollars. Judge Barker was appointed in 1984 and served until 2001. Before the appointment, she served as a United States District Attorney from 1977 to 1981. Before the U.S. Attorney appointment, Barker was in private law practice in downtown Indianapolis, Indiana. During the late 1980s and early 1990s, she was in an excellent position as a district judge. Barker has tried numerous criminal and civil cases in her court, giving her a wealth of knowledge and experience. When the civil rights case of Fred Sanders and the city of Indianapolis was on the docket, Sarah Barker was the fairest judge to preside in such a case. By chance, she happened to be the presiding judge.

In U.S. District Courts, civil case juries can have six to twelve jurors, but the attorneys must agree. In civil cases, the jury's verdict must be by a unanimous vote. The juries' burden proof in civil cases is called a 'preponderance of the evidence.' A 'preponderance of the evidence' is when the scales of justice tip, one way or the other, and the tip can be ever so slight, either way. One way the verdict is guilty the other way is not guilty. Remember, it's just a tip of the scales. In criminal cases, juries must have twelve people. The burden of proof is 'proof beyond a reasonable doubt.' 'Proof beyond a reasonable doubt' is when the scales of justice fall to the bottom, either way. One side of the scale is guilty; the other side is not guilty. Decisions on a verdict have to be unanimous among all jurors.

In the civil rights lawsuit, Fred Sanders' attorney subpoenaed fourteen Indianapolis police officers. The officers received a subpoena to the U.S. District Court in downtown Indianapolis. The jury of seven deliberated a little more than eight hours and found for the plaintiff, Fred Sanders. They found six officers liable for violating his civil rights while clearing eight officers of the alleged 'code of silence' (O'Neil, November 24, 1992).

The civil lawsuit against the Indianapolis Police during the Matt Faber murder was a long-drawn-out process that started early in the morning with the jury selection process. Before the jury selection began for this trial, the plaintiff and defendant's lawyers agreed to a seven-member jury. It takes less time to select seven members compared to twelve. There must be one alternate juror selected for the civil suit and two alternates for the criminal trial. Therefore, cutting the jury selection to almost half the time as the criminal trials. The selected jury consisted of three women and four men. The process took nearly an hour and a half to impanel the jury. Opening statements by the plaintiff and defendant's attorneys proceeded the jury selection.

A Senseless Murder and the Indianapolis Police Department

Open statements in all trials, whether criminal or civil case attorneys for both sides, direct their comments to the jury. After all, the jury makes the critical decision in any case. They are the decision-makers and therefore pass judgment after all the evidence and testimony have been examined. The civil rights lawsuit is not a murder trial of Sanders. Mr. Shortridge represented Sanders' opening statement by painting a rosy picture of Fred Sanders by giving the jury the illusion he is an 'angel.' Shortridge said Sanders was at home minding his own business. The police show up at his front door, trying to force it open. Fred was simply defending himself from the police.

The defendants had two attorneys; 1) Jack Ruckelshaus 2) John Kautzman, who represented six Indianapolis police officers. Two patrol officers 1) Larry Fender, 2) Robert Ward, and four sergeants 1) Sergeant Knap, 2) Sergeant Sickels, 3) Sergeant Coleman, 4) Sergeant Upton. Kautzman led the opening by stating Officer Faber received a radio run on a complaint of dogs chasing kids in the neighborhood. Officer Faber met Perry Evans, who lived across the street from Fred Sanders. Evans complained Sanders allowed his dog to chase his son riding a scooter in the street. He wanted the police to talk to Sanders. Faber walked across the street to speak with Sanders, but Sanders refused to cooperate and headed toward his house. Officer Faber attempted to stop him but was unsuccessful. Other officers were called to the scene, and several minutes later, Sanders shot Officer Faber in the back.

The basis of the lawsuit focused on what transpired after Sanders shot Faber. Sanders postulated several officers used unnecessary force and police brutality while and after he was being handcuffed. Fred Sanders was the principal witness for the plaintiff, as he was the plaintiff. His court testimony was as follows. 'Officers hit me, kicked me, then kicked me in the head while another officer twisted my leg trying to break it. There was another officer who spits on me while one was standing on my ankle.' Sanders based his civil rights lawsuit on the theory of a 'code of silence' that existed in the Indianapolis Police Department. The theory postulated the four supervisors conspired to hide the truth of his alleged 'beating' and conspired together to keep it a secret.

Section 1983 Lawsuit – How to Bring a Civil Rights Claim

How does a person pursue a civil rights lawsuit in the United States? These lawsuits are at the federal level and must follow strict rules. Part of the federal penal code, section 1983, allows citizens to sue for violating citizens' civil rights. These cases are filed at the U.S. District Court level. A civil rights lawsuit can be filed under Section 1983 by a person whose civil rights were violated (SHouse California Law Group, July 26, 2021). A plaintiff can file these lawsuits against individuals violating the civil rights due to them acting 'under color of law.' Color of law means the agent violating someone's civil rights has to be working for a governmental agency, usually law enforcement or a similar organization. The violation can happen when the violator is on or off-duty. Usually, these events occur during the official capacity of their jobs (Gardner, 2021).

Section 1983 lawsuits are procedural tools that provide guidance to specific federal laws. The law gives federal district courts jurisdiction to hear these cases. No one person can be held liable in these courts. Instead, the law establishes liability for violating Section 1983 and other federal laws (SHouse California Law Group, July 26, 2021). Since most Section 1983 lawsuits are against people who work for governmental agencies, most of these agencies pay liability lawsuits, not the individual. Herein lies the reason why there are so many 1983 lawsuits. The payoff can be in the hundreds of thousands of dollars, if not millions. Typically 1983 lawsuits involve police misconduct such as unnecessary use of force, police brutality, or false arrest. Cases can include unreasonable search and seizure, illegal search, or official misconduct. These are examples of federal violations for which an individual can be found negligent and liable. There are several other liability issues. Remember, these are lawsuits, not criminal prosecutions. Therefore nobody goes to jail if they are held responsible. Defendants pay a judgment usually set by the court or jury. Both parties could reach a settlement agreed upon by both sides, and the rest is history.

A Senseless Murder and the Indianapolis Police Department

As the lawsuit proceeds and as with most civil lawsuits, the plaintiff usually presents their case first. When they have finished their case, the defense gives their side of the story. Once that is complete, sometimes the plaintiff may introduce 'rebuttal witnesses,' providing the judge allows this tactic. During this chapter, it is essential to know what transpired throughout the lawsuit by both parties; the plaintiff, Fred Sanders v the City of Indianapolis et al., let's explore how the plaintiff presented its case. The plaintiff called several witnesses, but we are concerned with a few 1) Fred Sanders, 2) William B. Head, an expert witness discussing the theoretical existence of a 'code of silence' in some police departments, 3) the psychiatrist called as an expert witness by Sanders, who testified that Sanders suffers a Post-Traumatic Stress Disorder (name unknown), 4) emergency room doctor from Wishard Memorial Hospital.

Tuesday, November 12, 1992, the *Indianapolis Star* published an article, 'Sanders wins civil rights suit against the police.' The story read, 'Sanders was awarded 1.5 million in damages Monday night by a U.S. District Court jury. They agreed with the plaintiff, Sanders. The police used excessive force when he was beaten on August 14, 1988. Jurors agreed three police officers used excessive force, and four supervisors "on the scene" failed to intervene to stop that abuse. The jury further said, "all six officers on the Sanders' scene corresponded with each other to cover up the abuse." The jury of three women and four men deliberated almost eight and a half hours; around 10:20 p.m., they reached a verdict. The verdict was read to the court, and Sanders was emotionless; he barely moved. Sanders said to reporters, "I was a bit surprised. I was relieved, mostly," he said. Sanders further said, "I didn't think I did good enough. It's tough in courtroom situations sometimes."' (O'Neill, November 24, 1992).

'Sanders won $550,000 for the use of excessive force from Ward, Fender, and Knap while they were trying to get into his house. Another $250,000 for excessive force by Ward and Fender after Faber was shot.' '$100,000 for each of the four supervisors (total $400,000) who failed to intervene during the alleged beating.' 'A total of $300,000 for the six officers keeping a "code of silence" and covering up after the incident to protect one another.' Eight other officers were named in the Sanders' lawsuit. Their names have not been discussed, but they have cleared the 'code of silence' allegation (O'Neill, November 24, 1992).

Attorney for the defense, John Kautzman, stated motions for a new trial and another asked Judge Barker to set aside the jury's verdict and find in favor of the defendants. The defense has ten days to file these motions. A city attorney, Joseph Perkins, said if an appeals court affirms the damages, the city will cover the award cost. Money to pay the award will come from the police department's budget. Robert Ward's liability is different than the other officers. He pleaded guilty to criminal charges stemming from the Sanders incident and resigned from the department shortly afterward. Previously Perkins said the city was not obligated to any judgment awarded against Ward for his criminal acts. A discussion regarding the matter needs to be aired out by the defense and city of Indianapolis (O'Neill, November 24, 1992).

'The award of 1.5 million is half of what the plaintiff was seeking. It is the highest the plaintiffs' counsel has ever received.' Douglas R. Shortridge said, 'I feel wonderful and vindicated. I'm wonderfully happy. I think the jury sent a message to the city.' In December 1990, Larry Fender was acquitted of criminal charges involving Fred Sanders. Fender said, 'We don't know why the jury chose to ignore the evidence.' In another message from the department's union, the Fraternal Order of Police Lodge 86. The President of the union, James Nash, said 'It's historic and tragic. It's a real trauma, trying to make decisions that police officers are trying to make every day. The impact of this tragedy will take a while to set in.' As for the Indianapolis Police Department, the jury's decision was a total shock to the rank and file of the organization (O'Neill, November 24, 1992).

Fred Sanders took the witness stand and testified during his lawsuit. Sanders said he was kicked and beaten by the police after mortally wounding Matt Faber on August 14, 1988. He made these statements, 'I was being kicked and hit and beaten all over my body. Various officers would come by, hit me, beat me, spit on me, swear at me. One officer picked my leg up and tried to twist it off. Another officer was standing on my ankle.' He also testified while the officers were trying to open his front door, he was being hit and sprayed with a chemical repellant as they tried to make their way into the house.

A Senseless Murder and the Indianapolis Police Department

During the time at the front door, Sanders said, he was in fear for his life and determined to defend his home (O'Neill, November 19, 1992).

As Matt Faber arrived at Perry Evans' home on August 14, 1988, Sanders stood in his front yard. Officer Faber came across the street and began talking to him while he (Sanders) was in his yard. Sanders made the following statement, while the two were in the front yard, Sanders said of Officer Faber, 'He said if he had to come back, he'd shoot the dog himself. I was a little startled. I asked if he was finished. He said yes. I asked if I was under arrest. He said no.' Sanders said during cross-examination by the defense counsel, Faber did tell him not to go in the house. Sanders continued toward the house, and he said, 'I started walking quickly towards my house. I tried to close the door, but he came forward and put his foot in the door.' Faber asked Sanders, 'Come on outside, and we will talk.' Sanders commented, 'I don't want to talk to you anymore.' Shortly afterward, Sergeant Knap and officer Larry Fender arrived at the front door (O'Neill, November 19, 1992).

Under cross-examination by defense attorney Jack Ruckelshaus, Fred Sanders was asked, 'Why did you pick up the shotgun?' Sanders replied, 'It was a natural reflex on my part to stop the police.' Ruckelshaus asked, 'What was the purpose of getting the shotgun?' Sanders replied, 'To stop these officers.' Response from Ruckelshaus, 'To shoot 'em? Is that right?' Sanders replied, 'Yes' (O'Neill, November 19, 1992).

While in his house on August 14, 1988, the shotgun was in the bedroom where Sanders retrieved it. From his testimony provides the following information. 'After grabbing the shotgun, I came around the corner (from the kitchen), and Faber saw the shotgun; he turned around like he was heading for the door. I brought the shotgun up, and it went off, striking him in the back.' A few seconds later. 'I felt pain in my left leg.' Sanders learned later that evening he had been shot. Fred went on to say he thinks the police fired their guns the same time as he fired the shotgun. During an interview with defense attorney Jack Ruckelshaus, he represented Fender as his defense counsel in the criminal charges filed against him for the beating of

Sanders. During that trial, during Sanders' sworn testimony, Sanders said he fired the shotgun first (O'Neill, November 19, 1992).

Defense Witnesses

The chief witnesses for the defense were the officers and supervisors showing up at the scene. The witnesses are; Sergeants; 1) Knap, 2) Sickels, 3) Coleman, 4) Upton, Officers; 1) Ward, 2) Fender. Of the four supervisors, there was not much difference in their testimony. There's a reason this occurred, except for Sergeant Knap, who was the first to arrive at Sanders' residence. He was there within two minutes of the call for assistance. The remainder were Sickels, Coleman, and Upton. Coleman and Upton were the second units to arrive after Knap and Larry Fender. Sickels was the last supervisor to arrive at Sanders' residence. He arrived at Sanders' residence more than ten minutes after the communications branch reported the shooting. Coleman and Upton came about ten minutes after the shooting. That leaves Kent Knap at the scene when everything happens.

Kent witnessed Matt get shot in the back by Fred Sanders. He and Larry Fender fired their guns at Sanders several times. It was discovered later one of them shot Sanders in the left leg and face. Both Knap and Fender were active participants in the police action shooting. They were not bystanders watching a movie. They took an active role at the crime scene. Seconds after the shooting, Sanders gives up and comes outside. As he walks out the door, he sees Sergeant Knap and shoved him down into the bushes by the porch. Other officers nearby grabbed Sanders and led him to the front yard, and handcuffed him. The described situation took active officers to play a role in getting something done with Sanders. Everything that occurred had witnesses that someone could explain.

It's a different story regarding the presents of sergeants Sickels, Coleman, and Upton. These sergeants came to Sanders' residence ten to fifteen minutes after the shooting. By the time they arrived, ambulances and fire rescue were working on Officer Faber's wound and preparing Sanders for a ride to the hospital. Sergeant Sickels was responsible for completing the supervisor reports for the incident. Coleman and Upton ran crime scene tape to set up a perimeter around Sanders' residence. If Sanders was abused or beaten by the police, it happened before Sickels, Coleman, and Upton arrived. Contrary to the jury's ruling, they didn't believe the sergeants' courtroom testimony. In statements from a few of the jurors, it was said, 'Since they were there, they must have seen something. Therefore they are covering up or hiding the facts. So, there must be a "code of silence" case' (O'Neill, November 19, 1992).

All four sergeants testified during the lawsuit, and they pretty much said the same thing. Neither of them saw the abuse of power, police brutality, unnecessary use of force, hitting, kicking, spitting, name-calling, pulling legs and stepping on ankles, or anything else police officers should not do to crime suspects. Supervisors receive training to ensure subordinates conform to department rules and regulations, standard operating procedures, and the bible, which goes by the name of 'General Orders.' Supervisors are required to intervene in situations where officers use force on suspects and reach their limits. Supervisors ensure subordinates comply with department rules and regulations. It's their job.

Judge Barker's Ruling on the Verdict
December 24, 1992

William B. Head, a college professor, gave his testimony on the theory and reality of a 'code of silence' existing in some police departments. He was a witness for the plaintiff, Sanders, and his presence was for their benefit. The critical comment made by Mr. Head was he did not have any proof or evidence that a 'code of silence' exists for the Indianapolis Police Department. William did not benefit the Sanders team at all. When cross- examined by the defendants' counsel, he did not provide any testimony to support such a claim (Sanders v. City of Indianapolis, 837 F. Supp. 959 S.D. Ind. 1992)

The psychiatrist called as a witness for Sanders wasn't helpful either. He was able to cite Sanders did suffer a bout of 'Post-Traumatic Stress Disorder.' This condition caused Sanders to have insomnia, headaches, nightmares, and fear of authority since the shooting occurred. The psychiatrist did not establish Sanders had long-term effects from the disorder, nor did he have to be medicated or have ongoing medical treatment of 'post-traumatic stress disorder.' Again this witness did not provide help for the Sanders team. The only topic developed by the psychiatrist was the fact Fred Sanders was identified as having a few episodes of the disorder. Having this disorder did not cost Sanders money because he was treated for the stress while being detained at Wishard Memorial Hospital. The cost for treating post-traumatic stress disorder was paid by the city of Indianapolis. Therefore, Sanders' psychological injuries are not unlike the physical injuries in that they are compensable only based on the "pain and suffering" Sanders has experienced (Sanders v. City of Indianapolis, 837 F. Supp. 959 S.D. Ind. 1992).

The court had difficulty believing the jury's decision. The jury had to decide the Sanders case solely on the evidence presented was its decision to award Sanders a total of 1.5 million dollars in *compensatory* damages. All of Sanders' compensable injuries were 'intangible.' His injuries were: two scalp wounds his head felt as if it had been 'bashed-in,' (but x-rays revealed no skull fracture); a somewhat serious, but non-blinding eye wound; some soft tissue injuries; a broken leg (from which he occasionally limps); and a broken knuckle, a 'boxer's fracture.' Therefore, the physical injuries Sanders sustained are only compensable in terms of 'pain and suffering' (Sanders v. City of Indianapolis, 837 F. Supp. 959 S.D. Ind. 1992).

In its decision, the court recognizes the difficulty in pinning down an exact dollar amount. An award of 1.5 million dollars for the type of non- permanently disabling physical injuries Sanders suffered is exaggerated to the point of bearing no relationship to the evidence presented at trial. 'The amount of this verdict is excessive beyond reason; it is outrageous, shocking the conscience of this Court.' These were the words of Judge Barker in her brief of the jury's decision. 'The jury exceeded its charge when it acted to punish the individual defendant police officers. It was not its duty, nor was it lawfully authorized, to "send a message" to all police officers that excessive force would not be tolerated. Such a damage award can only be understood as a form of punishment and vindictiveness. The jury exceeded its charge when it acted to punish the individual defendant police officers' (Sanders v. City of Indianapolis, 837 F. Supp. 959 S.D. Ind. 1992).

Judge Barker found it challenging to understand why a jury could approve such a decision, especially when instructed to the laws governing their decision-making process. 'This verdict so far surpassed its evidentiary basis; one cannot help but wonder whether the larger national social and political climate entered into the thinking of individual jurors. They sought to counter-balance other perceived wrongs to other citizens by other police officers in other places. Whatever the jury's rationale, one thing is clear: they most assuredly abandoned their sworn duty to determine damages following the evidence and the Court's instructions on the applicable law' (Sanders v. City of Indianapolis, 837 F. Supp. 959 S.D. Ind. 1992).

The Judgment of Officer Ward

The jury returned an award of $50,000 against Robert Ward for the excessive force used against Fred Sanders. These events occurred inside of the front door before the shooting. Yet, the trial evidence regarding the area just inside the front door does not support this verdict. Officer Ward was assisting other officers who were trying to gain entry at the front door. Officer Ward used excessive force after the shooting while Sanders lay handcuffed on his front lawn. Since the door did not open, Ward decided to go to the back door. Sanders' group did not present evidence that Ward abused Sanders while assisting officers at the front door (Sanders v. City of Indianapolis, 837 F. Supp. 959 S.D. Ind. 1992).

'No reasonable jury could find that Officer Ward's actions in merely pushing on, but not moving, a door was excessive, especially when it is uncontroverted that the person behind the door, according to the information provided by his fellow officers, was committing the crime of resisting arrest.' Additionally, the plaintiff did not present evidence he was injured resulting from officer Wards' actions, pushing the front door. 'As a matter of law, a jury could reasonably reach a verdict against Officer Ward concerning the allegations that he used excessive force at and or immediately inside Sanders' front door.' The court granted the motion and 'Officer Ward's conduct at or immediately inside Sanders' front door, and that portion of the verdict against Officer Ward is vacated' (Sanders v. City of Indianapolis, 837 F. Supp. 959 S.D. Ind. 1992).

Judgments Against Conspiracy Defendants, Knap, Sickels, Coleman, Upton, Ward, and Fender

The jury found all six officers liable for their actions. Each of the officers had conspired with one another to conceal evidence, denying Sanders' First Amendment 'right-of-access' to the courts. Those verdicts cannot stand because Sanders did not present any evidence to support his conspiracy theory. Sanders' allegation to the 'code of silence' conspiracy theory. The six officers were together during Sanders' beating while he was on the ground. All officers joined in the conspiracy to hide the identities of the officers involved in the alleged beating. The real purpose of the conspiracy was to deny Sanders free access to the court system (Sanders v. City of Indianapolis, 837 F. Supp. 959 S.D. Ind. 1992).

The judge instructed the jury on several essential points. 'A conspiracy exists when two or more people reach an understanding to accomplish some unlawful purpose or to accomplish some lawful purpose by unlawful means.' So, a conspiracy is a kind of partnership in which each member becomes the agent of every other member. The essence of a conspiracy is a combination or agreement to violate or to disregard the law. 'Mere similarity of conduct among various persons and the fact that they may have associated with each other and may have assembled together and may have discussed some common aims and interests is not necessarily proof of the existence of a conspiracy' (Sanders v. City of Indianapolis, 837 F. Supp. 959 S.D. Ind. 1992).

'The evidence in the case need not show that the members entered into any express or formal agreement, or that they directly, by words spoken or in writing, stated between themselves what their object or purpose was to be, or the details thereof, or how the object or purpose was to be accomplished. To establish that a conspiracy existed, the plaintiff must show that members of the conspiracy in some way or manner, or through some contrivance, positively or tacitly came to a mutual understanding to accomplish a common and unlawful plan.' 'A person may become a member of a conspiracy without full knowledge of all the details of the conspiracy. A person who has no knowledge of a conspiracy but happens to act in a way that furthers some object or purpose of the conspiracy does not thereby become a conspirator' (Sanders v. City of Indianapolis, 837 F. Supp. 959 S.D. Ind. 1992).

'The key element in Sanders' cover-up claim is that officers of the Indianapolis Police Department conspired to hide or withhold from Sanders evidence of what happened on August 14, 1988, and as a result, Sanders could not bring his civil rights claim and be denied access to the courts. However, Sanders failed to put forth any evidence to establish that between August 14, 1988, and the time of trial, any conspirator defendant hid, concealed, or withheld evidence concerning the events of August 14, 1988. Sanders presented no evidence of non-responsive affidavits, interrogatories, or depositions from the defendants' (Sanders v. City of Indianapolis, 837 F. Supp. 959 S.D. Ind. 1992).

'Sanders' evidence was limited to a showing that the conspirator defendants when on the witness stand, neither saw, spoke, nor heard any "evil." As such, Sanders' "code of silence" claim was simply that the police officers conspired to commit perjury, and therein lies its flaw, because a witness' false or misleading sworn testimony cannot form the basis for a 1983 liability. As Sanders called Sergeants Knapp, Upton, Sickels, and Coleman, and Officers Ward and Fender, each testified that he was present at Sanders house at some point on August 14, 1988, but did not see anyone (including Officers Ward or Fender) use excessive force against Sanders while Sanders was on his porch or front lawn. As to these points, Sanders failed to present any discrediting or rebuttal evidence. This claim must therefore be vacated' (Sanders v. City of Indianapolis, 837 F. Supp. 959 S.D. Ind. 1992).

'Another issue with the conspiracy theory. Conspiracy evidence is the critical element of the agreement between two or more conspiracy defendants to conceal evidence. Though Sanders called an expert witness (William B. Head) who testified as to the theoretical existence of a "code of silence" in some police departments, Sanders presented no evidence of a "code of silence" in the Indianapolis Police Department; Professor Head explicitly testified that he had no knowledge of such a code within the Indianapolis Police Department. Sanders failed to present any discrediting or rebuttal evidence. The conspiracy claim had no evidentiary basis whatsoever. He required the jury to speculate that, because the defendant police officers were present at Sanders' house on August 14, 1988, they "must" have seen something, and since they are police officers and "must" have seen something, they "must" have conspired to conceal what they saw. Such speculation, however, is not evidence. Because a verdict based only on speculation cannot stand as a matter of law, these conspiracy verdicts must be set aside' (Sanders v. City of Indianapolis, 837 F. Supp. 959 S.D. Ind. 1992).

A code of silence verdict. 'A verdict based on the assumption that police officers, on every occasion, conspire to conceal evidence is akin to the conclusion that all mechanics, when they have the opportunity, assess overcharges for unnecessary repairs; that all politicians, when the public's back is turned, accept bribes; and that all taxpayers, when they think they can get anyway with it, cheat on their taxes and no one ever tells. This Court would no more permit a conviction for tax evasion based on speculation and opportunity to stand than it would allow what appears to be a verdict born of nothing more than prejudicial assumptions against the alleged co-conspirator defendants in this case; to stand. Simply put, there was no evidence, direct or circumstantial, sufficient to support a reasonable inference of an unlawful agreement, never mind unlawful agreement to deny Sanders' right of access to the courts. Since the verdict is not supported by the evidence presented at trial, the motion for judgment as a matter of law for the conspirator defendants must be granted' (Sanders v. City of Indianapolis, 837 F. Supp. 959 S.D. Ind. 1992).

Judgments Against the Supervisors' Sergeants Knap, Sickels, Coleman, Upton.

'As was true with the above discussed "code of silence" theory, Sanders did not present evidence that Sergeants Knapp, Coleman, Sickels, or Upton saw anyone (including Ward or Fender) exert or apply excessive force against him. As the Court instructed the jury, to prevail on this claim, Sanders had to prove that: 1) a defendant knew that a fellow officer was inflicting excessive or unreasonable force upon the plaintiff and 2) the supervising defendant had both the time and the present ability to intervene and prevent further harm to the plaintiff. Sanders presented no evidence as to either element to any of these defendants. According to the Court's review of the trial evidence, each of these sergeants testified that he did not see anyone (including Officers Ward or Fender) utilize excessive force against Sanders' (Sanders v. City of Indianapolis, 837 F. Supp. 959 S.D. Ind. 1992).

'Sanders failed to present evidence sufficient to support his claim that any of these supervising officers could prevent a fellow officer's use of excessive force. No evidence from police officers, non-police officers, from the media, or Sanders himself refuted the testimony of these supervisory officers. Whether Officers Ward or Fender or some other officer exerted excessive force again is not the issue here; the relevant inquiry is whether the supervisory officers *saw* a fellow officer apply excessive force and whether, when they saw it, they could *stop* the use of that force and *failed* to do so' (Sanders v. City of Indianapolis, 837 F. Supp. 959 S.D. Ind. 1992).

'Sanders' "failure to intervene" claim, like the "code of silence" claim, was based purely on speculation, speculation that ran something like this: because police officers were at his house on August 14, 1988, they "must" have seen someone apply excessive force, and, since they "must" have seen someone apply excessive force, they "must" have been able to prevent that application of force. A verdict based only on such assumptions and speculation cannot stand. Accordingly, the motion for judgment as a matter of law is granted as it pertains to the "failure to intervene" defendants' (Sanders v. City of Indianapolis, 837 F. Supp. 959 S.D. Ind. 1992).

Motion for a New Trial or Remittitur

The defendant's attorneys, Jack Ruckelshaus and John Kautzman, filed the motion for remittitur. What is it? What is a remittitur? A procedure under which a court may order the reduction of an excessive verdict. A procedure in which the court requires the plaintiff to remit a portion of the judgment deemed excessive instead of a grant of a defendant's motion for a new trial or a reversal if the court is an appellate court (*Findlaw Dictionary*, January 2021).

'Perhaps more troubling than the jury's above-discussed disregard of its duty to decide this case based solely on the evidence presented was its decision to award Sanders a total of 1.5 million dollars in *compensatory* damages. Compensatory damages are such damages as will compensate the injured party for the injury sustained and nothing more. All of Sanders' compensable injuries were "intangible." Sanders suffered compensable physical injuries on August 14, 1988: two scalp wounds (Sanders testified that at or shortly after the incident in question, his head felt as if it had been "bashed-in," but x-rays revealed no skull fracture); a somewhat serious, but non-blinding eye wound; some soft tissue injuries; a broken leg (from which he occasionally limps); and a broken knuckle (a "boxer's fracture"). However, because Sanders was arrested and taken into police custody on August 14, 1988, Sanders received medical treatment for those (and other) injuries from the largesse of the state and was not personally charged for the costs of that treatment. In short, Sanders suffered no medical bills from the events of August 14, 1988, and Sanders' physical injuries are therefore only compensable in terms of "pain and suffering"' (Sanders v. City of Indianapolis, 837 F. Supp. 959 S.D. Ind. 1992). You were wondering, define largesse of the state? The generous bestowal of gifts, favors, or money (*Findlaw Dictionary*, January 2021).

'It is clear that an award of 1.5 million dollars for the type of non- permanently disabling physical injuries Sanders suffered is exaggerated to the point of bearing no relationship to the evidence presented at trial. The amount of this verdict is excessive beyond reason; it is outrageous, shocking the conscience of this Court. The jury, who was not permitted to award punitive damages, assessed liability in one instance at nearly one-half a million dollars against a single, individual officer (Sergeant Knap). Such a damage award can only be understood as a form of punishment and vindictiveness. The jury exceeded its charge when it acted to punish the individual defendant police officers. It was not its duty, nor was it lawfully authorized, to "send a message" to all police officers that excessive force will not be tolerated' (Sanders v. City of Indianapolis, 837 F. Supp. 959 S.D. Ind. 1992).

Judges Review: Concluding

'The issues presented to the jury, in this case, were narrow and well- defined. They did not include every conceivable theory of recovery either because the Court had previously ruled that they were unsupported by the evidence or because Sanders, himself, had voluntarily decided to withdraw them. The Court's instructions to the jury presented the only theories upon which Sanders could lawfully recover. The jurors had no license to deviate from these instructions, to supplement them with their own notions of what the applicable law should be, or to speculate about the existence or compensability of other injuries' (Sanders v. City of Indianapolis, 837 F. Supp. 959 S.D. Ind. 1992).

'Although the precise course and rationale of the jury's deliberations remain beyond the Court's actual knowledge, it is evident that the jury's results are so detached from the controlling legal principles, and the evidence presented that the Court has virtually no choice but to make the ruling it has in this entry made. Regrettably, from everyone's perspective, the jurors turned to their instincts for guidance, and the result is a verdict motivated by vengeance, passion, or benevolence, a verdict clearly beyond their lawful commission and charter' (Sanders v. City of Indianapolis, 837 F. Supp. 959 S.D. Ind. 1992).

'The motion for judgment as a matter of law, as it pertains to the claim that Officer Ward used excessive force at and immediately inside Sanders' front door before the shooting, the "code of silence"/ conspiracy claim, and the "failure to intervene" claim, is GRANTED. In addition, for the reasons stated above, the Court GRANTS the motion for remittitur or a new trial on the remaining claims' (Sanders v. City of Indianapolis, 837 F. Supp. 959 S.D. Ind. 1992).

Conclusion

Matt Faber began his law enforcement career when he was twenty-two years old. A career he wanted so much, he could taste it. Before becoming a police officer, his girlfriend Jan was an Indianapolis Police Officer. They met while Matt was going to Indiana University, Indianapolis. He was a physical education major in the School of Education. After completing his degree, he would be qualified as a physical education instructor in public schools. However, he didn't want that type of job. Before graduating from college, he applied to the Indianapolis Police Department. He received his degree close to the same time; the Indianapolis Police Department hired him as a recruit trainee. All newly hired recruit trainees will attend the Indianapolis Police Academy for more than eleven months.

The author of this book has decided to put this story in a book to get people to read what really happened to Matt Faber. Matt was young and had a long career ahead. At the beginning of his career, he was still learning the details of being a good police officer. He had been in the Department for fourteen months, that's a bit over four months beyond the Indianapolis Police Academy training. That's just starting to scratch the surface of police officer experience. A well-experienced officer takes years of work to achieve. The time takes so long because some police work is routine and not challenging. When these tasks do occur, more complicated tasks have sizable gaps between challenging assignments. Otherwise, challenging tasks are few and far between.

Like all new officers, Matt was no different. New officers want to show their skills and are eager to impress veteran officers and their supervisors. They want to do something even if it's wrong. New officers may get their feelings hurt more quickly than others if they make an error. But most will bounce back soon. They are impressionable and have a desire to learn. These were the traits Matt possessed. During the four months the author had the privilege to know him, Matt exceeded all expectations of a new officer. He had a desire to do well and do things right. The author felt it was a pleasure talking to him and having those long conversations together. He has been missed over the past thirty-three years, and he will continue to be missed.

During and after Matt was murdered by Fred Sanders, to this date, the author still has a terrible taste in his mouth about Fred Sanders and the murder he escaped. He is nothing but a scumbag murderer that should have been charged with felony murder and executed by now. Instead, Sanders is a free man. This author wrote a book about a rape case he investigated when he was a sex crimes detective. The alleged victim was a sixteen-year-old liar and accused a thirty-three-year-old man of rape and armed robbery. He always maintained his innocence. He was convicted and sentenced to forty years in the Indiana State Prison for a crime he did not commit. He served almost eight years in prison for the alleged crime until he was released from DNA tests results. His name was Dwayne Scruggs. Book title: *Rape. I'm Innocent. I Didn't Do It*.

Scruggs did not commit the crime but spent almost eight years more in the Indiana State Prison for a crime he did not commit. Sanders murders a police officer by shooting him in the back and serves just three years in jail, but he never saw a prison. He spent time in a diagnostic center, a mental health facility run by the Department of Corrections. Where is justice in this scenario? Matt's murder has to go down in record as Indianapolis' worse case in history, bar none! The Faber case spun out of control because two officers were charged with misdemeanor charges of battery because they hit Fred Sanders while he was being handcuffed. After the officers assaulted Sanders, he was not injured from the event. Fred Sanders pleaded guilty to involuntary manslaughter because Marion County Prosecutor Stephen Goldsmith ran for Mayor of Indianapolis. It was Goldsmith's agreement with Sanders' criminal defense attorney.

Earlier in this writing, there was a discussion about Matt Faber and his wife Jan talking about their separation and impending divorce, which never happened. There were other issues regarding the couple that came to light. However, after the shooting incident by Fred Sanders, things may have changed. Matt's death may have triggered some degree of emotion that has lasted a lifetime with Jan Faber. She has dedicated part of her life to recognizing Matt's contribution and dedication towards law enforcement and the Indianapolis Police Department. She had the memorial erected (below) in Matt's name.

'In December 2011, twenty-three years after the death of Patrol Officer Faber, his wife (a sergeant with the department) dedicated a memorial to him outside the building where he had reported to duty. Besides a large boulder engraved on his badge number, the date he was sworn in, and the day he died, is a sturdy bench and a new tree' (Indianapolis Police Department, August 23, 2021). About her husband, Sergeant Faber said:

Photograph of the memorial. (Indianapolis Police Department, August 23, 2021).

'It's a way to honor him every day and keep his memory alive as long as possible, a proud officer, a man dedicated to his job, a man with a big heart, and also a comedian in any room. Someone Indianapolis should never forget.' (Jan Faber, 2021)

A photograph where Fred Sanders used to live today is an empty lot. The house was demolished years ago. There were too many bad memories at that site. Destroying the house was the best thing that could have happened to the premises. The lot is small, but the house is smaller. Hard to believe it was there at one time and is now gone.

Photograph (Indianapolis Police Department, August 23, 2021).

Matt Faber's headstone. West Ridge Park Cemetery 9295 West 21st Street Indianapolis, Indiana Garden of Devotion, Lot 167.

Headstone Photograph (Indianapolis Police Department, August 23, 2021).

Matt John Faber

The Indianapolis Police Department's Identification Branch took the photograph of Matt Faber during the first year he was hired.

A Senseless Murder and the Indianapolis Police Department

Attached Figures Below

INDIANAPOLIS POLICE DEPARTMENT

To: Chief Paul Annee
From: Sergeant Tommy Sickels
Subject: RESISTING ARREST – Supervisor's Report
Date: August 14th., 1988
Case No. 551478FA

Sir:

On 14th day, August 19 88 at 2140 hours, I investigated a resisting arrest incident. The following are the results of my investigation:

Day, Date, and Time of Incident: 14th day, August 1988 2140 hours
Location of Incident: 2968 Arthington Blvd.
Type of Premises: Residence
Type of Resistance: Physical X Weapon X Other (Explain)
CS Used: Yes X No Baton Used: Yes No X Other Defensive Weapon (Explain) Service Revolvers

OFFICERS INVOLVED:
- Matthew John Faber — Ident. No. F-2021 — Assignment Boy Tact
- Sgt. Kent Knap — Ident. No. X-4882 — Assignment Boy Tact
- Larry Fender — Ident. No. E-2674 — Assignment Boy Tact

WITNESSES:
- Perry Evans — Address 2961 N. Arthington Blvd., Phone 547-3634

ARRESTED:
- Fred C. Sanders — ED: H/NH Race B/W/I/O Sex M Age 44
- DOB 10-11-43 SSN 312-44-9633 Address 2968 Arthington Blvd.,
- Court Crim 6 Date 8-15-88 Time 1:30 PM
- Charges 3 Cts Attempt Murder; Battery PO W/Serious Injury Sent To: Wishard
- Conveyance Ambulance Injury Information Gunshot Wounds; Chest and legs.

Reporting Supervisor: Tommy Sickels Rank Sergeant Ident. No. S-2893
Commanding Officer: James Toler Rank Major Ident. No. T-5992

(Figure 1 Resisting Arrest Report Form. Pg. 1 of 2)

RELATED REPORTS ATTACHED (IF APPLICABLE):

☒ Officer Assaulted (IPD Form No. 1-1-44)

☒ Injured Officers Report (IPD Form No. 6-4-40)

☐ Request For Medical Services (IPD Form No. 1-1-62 R2)

☒ Use of CS Repellent Report (IPD Form No. 6-6-24 R1)

NARRATIVE: The narrative shall be very specific and include all pertinent information, facts, and a detailed account of the incident. (Use additional sheets if necessary.)

Officer Faber B-429 received a call to go to 2961 N. Arthington Blvd reference talking to a complainant, Perry Evans about Mr. Sanders dogs. Officer Faber was informing Mr. Sanders of the regulations pertainint to dogs in Marion County, but Sanders refused to cooperate. Officer Faber redioed for assistance. Sgt. Knap and Officer Fender Arrived. While trying to affect arrest on Sanders, Sanders ran into his house, and slammed the door in their faces. AS the officers forced open the front door, Officer Faber grabbed Sanders, Sanders being sweaty, Officer Faber slipped off him, and fell to the floor. At that time Sanders went into his bedroom located on the S/W part of the house and got a shotgun firing one shot at Officer Faber striking him in the upper portion of his back on the left side. At that time both Sgt. Knap and Officer Fender fired shots at Sanders. Sgt. Knap said he heard another shot. Officers Robert Ward, Marcus Kennedy, and James Harris went to the rear of the house. Officer Ward entered the back door and heard what he though to be a cocking of a gun. He then exited the house. He heard a gunshot and then noticed that his hand was bleeding, and cut in several places. Sgt. Knap said he knew that he had shot Sanders, and ordered him to come out. Sanders came out of the house, and was immediately handcuffed.

Prior to the officers entering the front door Officer Fender sprayed a long blast of CS Repellent at Sanders as he was hidding behind the door. The repellent had no effect on Sanders at all. Sanders was yelling obscenites and threatening the officers. Perry Evans had explained to Officer Faber earlier that Sanders has guns, and that he shot at his (Evans') house earlier this year. Faber had informed the other officers that Sanders may have a gun in the house prior to their entry.

It is my opinion that all officers involved in this incident acted properly and within departmental guidelines. Officers returning gunfire at Sanders did so in self defense. Sgt. Knap stated after Sanders shot Officer Faber, he (Sanders) pointed the shot gun at both him, and Officer Fender. They returned gunfire at Sanders as he hid behind a doorway leading to his bedroom, and he kept peeking out aiming the gun at them.

Detailed inter-departmentals are being prepared by homicide investigators assigned to this case that will detail the facts of this case.

(Figure 2 Resisting Arrest Report Form. Pg. 2 of 2)

A Senseless Murder and the Indianapolis Police Department

(Figure 3 Officer Assaulted Report Form)

```
                    DEPARTMENT OF PUBLIC SAFETY
                         POLICE DEPARTMENT
                        CITY OF INDIANAPOLIS

    REPORT OF PERSONAL INJURY TO POLICE OFFICER WHILE IN THE PERFORMANCE OF HIS DUTY

    (INSTRUCTIONS: This report is to be executed by, or in behalf of, any policeman who suffers an injury while performing
    his duty and is to be turned into the office of the chief of police within 24 hours after time of injury. If impossible for in-
    jured to execute this form, the partner or superior officer of such policeman shall execute same in his behalf and turn it in
    to said office within said period.)

    NAME OF OFFICER INJURED  Matthew John Faber            HOME ADDRESS 2805 Grassy Creek Dr.
    RANK  Patrolman       POSITION HELD Patrol Officer     AGE 24    PHONE NO. 894-4383
    DIVISION ASSIGNED TO  Operations                       HOURS OF DUTY 1900-0300
    DATE OF INJURY 8-14-88                                 TIME OF INJURY 9:35 PM
    LOCATION OR PLACE OF ACCIDENT 2968 N. Arthington Blvd.
    WHERE WAS OFFICER WORKING AT TIME OF ACCIDENT  Boy Quadrant
    HOW LONG ON DEPARTMENT 14 months     COMMANDING OFFICER Major James Toler
    ON ACTIVE DUTY AT TIME OF ACCIDENT? YES  X    NO
    DESCRIBE PARTICULAR ASSIGNMENT AT THE TIME OF ACCIDENT  Quad II TacT Shift

    DESCRIBE MANNER IN WHICH ACCIDENT OCCURRED  Responding to trouble with neighbors complaints
       of dogs at 2968 N. Arthington Blvd. Officer Faber was shot in the back with a
       shotgun by Fred Sanders, living at that address.
    DESCRIBE NATURE OF INJURY Wound to upper left back.
    DESCRIBE ANY TREATMENT OR CARE RECEIVED  Immediate surgery at Wishard E.R.
    NAME OF ATTENDING PHYSICIAN
    PROBABLE LENGTH OF DISABILITY Unknown
    WAS ANYONE TO BLAME FOR THE ACCIDENT  Fred Sanders
    WAS INJURED OFFICER NEGLECTFUL BY NOT OBSERVING SAFETY RULES AND REGULATIONS OF CITY ORDINANCES  No

    WAS INJURED SENT TO THE HOSPITAL, IF SO, WHICH ONE AND BY WHOM SENT  Officer Faber to Wishard Hospital

    NAMES OF ALL PERSONS, OR EMPLOYEES OF THE DEPARTMENT, WHO MAY HAVE KNOWLEDGE OF THE CIRCUMSTANCES OF
    THE ACCIDENT, OR WITNESSES TO SAME  Sgt. Knapp, Officers; Fender, L. Ward, R., Kennedy M.,
       and Harris J.
    I HEREBY CERTIFY, THIS  14th     DAY OF   August         19 88 . THAT THE ABOVE FACTS ARE
    TRUE TO THE BEST OF MY INFORMATION AND BELIEF.
    SIGNED  Tommy Sickels                       RANK  Sergeant
    POLICE SURGEON NOTIFIED                     BY
                                                                    (PD Form No. 4-4-40)
```

(Figure 4 Officer Injured Report Form)

A Senseless Murder and the Indianapolis Police Department

INDIANAPOLIS POLICE DEPARTMENT
CS REPELLENT USAGE

Case #: 551478PA
CAD #: 199930

Date of Use: 8-14-88   Time of Use: 9:34 PM   Location: 2968 N. Arthington Blvd.
Officer(s) Using CS Repellent: Larry Fender   F-2674   Quad II Tact Shift

Subject: Fred C. Sanders   W/M   10-11-43

Charges: 3 Cts. Attempted Murder; Resisting W/Deadly Weapon; Battery on Officer W/Deadly Weapon

Did CS Contact Subject's Nose? ☐ Yes ☑ No   If No, Point of Contact: General directional spray towards suspect as he was hidding behind a door.
Number of CS Bursts Sprayed: 1 long one   Officer's Distance from Subject: couple of feet

Effectiveness:
☐ Temporary Immobilization
☐ Minimal Effect
☑ Escalated Confrontation
☐ No Effect

Subject Condition:
☐ Normal
☐ Intoxicated Alcohol
☐ Intoxicated Drugs
☐ Mentally Disturbed
☑ Unknown
☐ Other

Environmental Condition:
☑ Indoor Use
☐ Rain
☐ High Winds
☐ Snow
☑ High Humidity
Temperature: 85 Degrees

If the CS had no effect or escalated the confrontation, list any factors contributing to its failure:
Probably due to the mental or emotional condition of the suspect in this incident.

Were any officers at the scene physically affected by the CS? ☑ Yes ☐ No
If yes, list names: Larry Fender   F2674   Quad II TAct

Other Methods of Control Used: ☐ None ☐ Baton ☐ Pressure Points ☑ Service Revolvers

Injury to Subject (Prior to and/or After Arrest): Subject was shot by officers after subject had shot officer Matthew John Faber in the back with a 12 guage shotgun

Special Reports Made: ☑ Yes ☐ No   Injured Officer's Report Made? ☑ Yes ☐ No

Brief Summary of Incident:
Officers were attempting to arrest subject, at which time subject went into his bedroom and got a shotgun which he used to shoot Officer Faber. CS was used while officers were trying to gain entry to the residence of the subject.

Reporting Supervisor: Tommy Sickels   Rank: Sergeant   ID#: 3-2893

IPD FORM NO. 6-8-24 R2

(Figure 5 CS Repellent Use Form)

Tommy Sickels

(Figure 6 Arrest Report Form)

A Senseless Murder and the Indianapolis Police Department

Indianapolis Metropolitan Police Department
GENERAL ORDER 1.1
LAW ENFORCEMENT ROLE AND RESPONSIBILITY

POLICY

The primary duty of a police officer is to uphold and enforce the law. Members of the Indianapolis Metropolitan Police Department must accept the responsibility of being held to a higher standard, and must be able to enforce the laws and protect the rights of its citizens. The application and enforcement of the law must be accomplished in the spirit set forth by the framers of the United States Constitution.

PROCEDURE

I. Oath of Office <1.1.1>

All persons employed by the Indianapolis Metropolitan Police Department as a merit or reserve police officer, prior to assuming sworn status, must meet with the Chief of Police to receive the oath of office for this department. The oath of office is as follows:

I, _____, do solemnly swear that I will support the Constitution of the United States and the Constitution of the State of Indiana, and I will faithfully discharge my duties as an officer of the Consolidated City of Indianapolis, under this appointment, according to law, and city ordinances, to the best of my ability, so help me God.

II. Legal Authority <1.2.1>

A. The Indianapolis Metropolitan Police Department is created and authorized under Section 279-102 of the "Revised Code of the Consolidated City and County" (As added G.O. No. 110, 2005) and IC 36-3-1-5.1.
B. Sworn officers are employees of the City of Indianapolis - Marion County and shall be assigned their duties by the Chief of Police or as required by law. There are two (2) categories of sworn officers.

　　1. Merit Officers; and
　　2. Reserve Officers

C. Each member of the department has the powers set forth in IC 36-8-3-6 (Powers and duties of Police Officers).

III. Authority to Carry and Use Weapons <1.2.2>

Sworn Officers are authorized to carry and use any weapon authorized and/or issued by the Indianapolis Metropolitan Police Department in the performance of their duties, so long as the officer has completed proficiency training authorized by the department and IC 5-2-1. (Mandatory Training for Law Enforcement Officers).

IV. Constitutional Rights <1.2.3>

A. It is the policy of the Indianapolis Metropolitan Police Department to comply with the highest standards of legal and professional conduct in dealing with a person's Constitutional Rights.

　　1. Officers will be mindful of the rights and protection afforded all persons by the United States Constitution and the Indiana Constitution.
　　2. Coercion or threats, real or implied, will not be used during interviews to obtain confessions. <1.2.3a>

PAUL R. CIESIELSKI
CHIEF OF POLICE

Supersedes IMPD General Order 1.1, Effective 05/05/09.

Effective: March 4, 2010
Page 1 of 2

(Figure 7 General Order 1.1)

About the Author

Dr. Tommy Sickels is a new author and decided to write books based on his personal experiences as a police officer. He served as a detective in the Sex Crimes Branch of the Indianapolis Police Department from 1983 to the fall of 1986. Other assignments included 1) Vice detective 2) motorcycle officer 3) Human resources specialist 4) Computer programmer 5) Data Processing Office Manager 6) District Sergeant. Dr. Sickels started his law enforcement career on February 8, 1975, through May 18, 1980 as a New Albany, Indiana police officer. The first three years as a patrol officer and the last two years as a supervising Corporal. He joined the Indianapolis Police Department on May 20, 1980 through December 3, 2007, when he retired with thirty-two years of law enforcement service.

In 2006, Tommy Sickels was one of eighteen appointed officers to the 'consolidation steering committee' selected by the Indianapolis Police Department and the Marion County Sheriff's Department. A year of committee's responsibilities included the following 1) Rewriting the Department's General Orders, 2) Rewriting the Rules and Regulations manual, 3) Rewriting the hiring and promotional processes, 4) Rewriting the disciplinary process, 5) Designing uniforms, car design, emblems, and the new department badge, 6) Developing academy and in-service training 7) Developing new Merit Board rules and regulations. This assignment took almost ten months to complete. The department implemented its new name, The Indianapolis Metropolitan Police Department, on January 1, 2007.

During the late 1980s, Sickels began teaching as an adjunct faculty member of criminal justice at Indiana University, Indianapolis, for a few years. During the middle 1990s, he began teaching as an adjunct criminal justice faculty member at Ivy Tech State College through 1999. He began teaching criminal justice for the University of Phoenix, where he taught until December 2018.

Education: Dr. Sickels completed the following degrees at Indiana University. Associate and bachelor's degrees. In the Graduate School of Public Administration, he completed the Certificate in Public Management (labor relations). The Graduate School of Public Affairs Sickels completed an MPA, Master of Public Administration – Double Major, Public Administration, and Criminal Justice. He graduated from the University of Phoenix with an Educational Doctorate Ed.D. Major – Leadership.

References

Bovsun, Mara. (January 23, 2019). "Mange in Dogs: What You Need to Know." American Kennel Club. https://www.akc.org/expert-advice/health/mange-what-you-need-to-know/

Findlaw Dictionary (January 2021). *Findlaw Dictionary*. https://dictionary.findlaw.com

Gardner, Bryan A. (2021). *Black's Law Dictionary*, 11th. Thompson West.

"How To Become A Police Officer." Website URL: https://www.how-to-become-a-police- officer.com/cities/indianapolis/

Indianapolis Police Department (August 23, 2021). "Pause and Remember Patrol Officer Matt J. Faber." Public Affairs Office.

Lewis, Sarah, Pharm. D. (February 6, 2020). "Medically Induced Coma." https://www.healthgrades.com /right-care/brain-and-nerves/medically-induced-coma

McClaren, George. (August 15, 1988). "Shooting Leaves IPD Officer in Critical Condition." *Indianapolis Star*, Indianapolis, Indiana.

Morgan, Kevin. (August 22, 1988). "Policeman Dies Nine Days After He Was Shot." *Indianapolis Star*, Indianapolis, Indiana.

Morgan, Kevin. (August 25, 1988) "Law Enforcement Salute Slain Patrolman." *Indianapolis Star*, Indianapolis, Indiana.

Rules and Regulations Manual. (2009). The Indianapolis Police Department Planning and Research Branch. Indianapolis, Indiana.

Sanders v. City of Indianapolis, 837 F. Supp. 959 Southern District Ind. 1992.

SHouse California Law Group. (July 26, 2021) https://www.shouselaw.com/ca/civil-rights/1983- lawsuits

Smith, Bruce. (August 22, 1988). "Police Mourn Death of Young Patrolman." *Indianapolis Star*, Indianapolis, Indiana.

O'Neil, R. John (November 24, 1992). "Sanders Says He Was

Kicked After He Shot Officer." *Indianapolis Star*, Indianapolis, Indiana.

O'Neill, R. John (November 24, 1992). "Sanders Wins Civil Rights Suit Against Police." *Indianapolis Star*, Indianapolis, Indiana.

Smith, Rob, (December 11, 1992). "Modisett is Seeking to Have Sanders Begin Serving Remaining Jail Sentence." Marion County Prosecuting Attorney.

Supreme Court of Indiana. 587 N.E.2d 166 (February 27, 1992).

Supreme Court of Indiana. 596 N.E.2d 225 (July 20, 1992). https://law.justia.com/cases/indiana/supreme-court/1992/49s02-9207-pc-563-4.html

Other Photos of Interest

(Indianapolis Star. August 15, 1988) Photo of paramedics taken close to Sanders' residence.

A Senseless Murder and the Indianapolis Police Department

(*Indianapolis Star*. August 25, 1988) The photo was taken in front of the Police Headquarters. 50 N. Alabama Street. Standing far left is Mayor William Hudnut.

(*Indianapolis Star*. Nov 17, 1992) Officer Larry Fender and Sergeant Kenneth Knap. Newspaper and other articles misspell his last name (Knapp). The photo was taken in U.S. District Court downtown Indianap

Milton Keynes UK
Ingram Content Group UK Ltd.
UKHW041007111124
451035UK00002B/380